LOST CIVILIZATIONS

THE HAN DYNASTY

Myra Immell

LUCENT BOOKS®

THOMSON

GALE

San Diego • Detroit • New York • San Francisco • Cleveland
New Haven, Conn. • Waterville, Maine • London • Munich

THOMSON

GALE

Picture Credits:

Cover Photo: © Erich Lessing/Art Resource
Bella Hollingworth, 24
© Bettmann/CORBIS, 51
© The Bridgeman Art Library, 8, 45, 80
© British Museum/The Bridgeman Art
    Library, 12
© Burnstein Collection/CORBIS, 57
© Pierre Colombel/CORBIS, 40
© CORBIS, 49, 52
© Werner Forman/Art Resource, 47, 68
© Giraudon/Art Resource, 11, 32, 44, 60

© Erich Lessing/Art Resource, 22, 30, 64
© NGS, 79
© Nimatallah/Art Resource, 6
North Wind Picture Archives, 69, 76
© Oriental Bronzes Ltd., London, 70
© PhotoDisc, 17
© Rèunion des Musèes, 41
© Royal Ontario Museum/CORBIS, 73
© Vanni/Art Resource, 14
© Roger Viollet/Hulton Archive, 37

Cover Photo: Life-size clay soldiers
line the tomb of Shi huangdi in Xian, China.

© 2003 by Lucent Books. Lucent Books is an imprint of The Gale Group, Inc.,
a division of Thomson Learning, Inc.

Lucent Books® and Thomson Learning™ are trademarks used herein under license.

For more information, contact
Lucent Books
27500 Drake Rd.
Farmington Hills, MI 48331-3535
Or you can visit our Internet site at http://www.gale.com

LIBRARY OF CONGRESS CATALOGING-IN-PUBLICATION DATA

Immell, Myra.
    The Han dynasty / Myra Immell.
    p.   cm. — (Lost civilizations)
    Summary: Discusses the Han Dynasty, their history, agriculture, government ,
and social structure.

Includes bibliographical references and index.

    ISBN 1-59018-096-8 (alk. paper)

    1. China—History—Han dynasty, 202 B.C.–A.D. 220—Juvenile literature.
I. Title.   II. Series.
    DS748 .I45 2003
    931'.04—dc21

                                                            2002003816

Printed in the United States of America

CONTENTS

FOREWORD

"What marvel is this?" asked the noted eighteenth-century German poet and philosopher, Friedrich Schiller. "O earth . . . what is your lap sending forth? Is there life in the deeps as well? A race yet unknown hiding under the lava?" The "marvel" that excited Schiller was the discovery, in the early 1700s, of two entire ancient Roman cities buried beneath over sixty feet of hardened volcanic ash and lava near the modern city of Naples, on Italy's western coast. "Ancient Pompeii is found again!" Schiller joyfully exclaimed. "And the city of Hercules rises!"

People had known about the existence of long lost civilizations before Schiller's day, of course. Stonehenge, a circle of huge, very ancient stones had stood, silent and mysterious, on a plain in Britain as long as people could remember. And the ruins of temples and other structures erected by the ancient inhabitants of Egypt, Palestine, Greece, and Rome had for untold centuries sprawled in magnificent profusion throughout the Mediterranean world. But when, why, and how were these monuments built? And what were the exact histories and beliefs of the peoples who built them? A few scattered surviving ancient literary texts had provided some partial answers to some of these questions. But not until Pompeii and Herculaneum started to emerge from the ashes did the modern world begin to study and re-

construct lost civilizations in a systematic manner.

Even then, the process was at first slow and uncertain. Pompeii, a bustling, prosperous town of some twenty thousand inhabitants, and the smaller Herculaneum met their doom on August 24, A.D. 79 when the nearby volcano, Mt. Vesuvius, blew its top and literally erased them from the map. For nearly seventeen centuries, their contents, preserved in a massive cocoon of volcanic debris, rested undisturbed. Not until the early eighteenth century did people begin raising statues and other artifacts from the buried cities; and at first this was done in a haphazard, unscientific manner. The diggers, who were seeking art treasures to adorn their gardens and mansions, gave no thought to the historical value of the finds. The sad fact was that at the time no trained experts existed to dig up and study lost civilizations in a proper manner.

This unfortunate situation began to change in 1763. In that year, Johann J. Winckelmann, a German librarian fascinated by antiquities (the name then used for ancient artifacts), began to investigate Pompeii and Herculaneum. Although he made some mistakes and drew some wrong conclusions, Winckelmann laid the initial, crucial groundwork for a new science—archaeology (a term derived from two Greek words meaning "to talk about ancient things"). His book, *History of the Art of Antiquity*, became a model for the first generation of archaeologists to follow in their efforts to understand other lost civilizations. "With unerring sensitivity," noted scholar C.W. Ceram explains, "Winckelmann groped toward original insights, and expressed them with such power of language that the cultured European world was carried away by a wave of enthusiasm for the antique ideal. This . . . was of prime importance in shaping the course of archaeology in the following century. It demonstrated means of understanding ancient cultures through their artifacts."

In the two centuries that followed, archaeologists, historians, and other scholars began to piece together the remains of lost civilizations around the world. The glory that was Greece, the grandeur that was Rome, the cradles of human civilization in Egypt's Nile valley and Mesopotamia's Tigris-Euphrates valley, the colorful royal court of ancient China's Han Dynasty, the mysterious stone cities of the Maya and Aztecs in Central America—all of these

and many more were revealed in fascinating, often startling, if sometimes incomplete detail by the romantic adventure of archaeological research. This work, which continues, is vital. "Digs are in progress all over the world," says Ceram. "For we need to understand the past five thousand years in order to master the next hundred years."

Each volume in the *Lost Civilizations* series examines the history, works, everyday life, and importance of ancient cultures. The archaeological discoveries and methods used to gather this knowledge are stressed throughout. Where possible, quotes by the ancients themselves, and also by later historians, archaeologists, and other experts support and enliven the text. Primary and secondary sources are carefully documented by footnotes and each volume supplies the reader with an extensive Works Consulted list. These and other research tools afford the reader a thorough understanding of how a civilization that was long lost has once more seen the light of day and begun to reveal its secrets to its captivated modern descendants.

THE GREAT HAN DYNASTY

In the summer of 1968, archaeologists excavated twin tombs hidden in caves cut deep into a rocky cliff at Lingshan in Mancheng County in China's Hebei province, about ninety miles from the modern-day city of Beijing. Created along an axis and arranged like buildings, the tombs represented a vast palace reproduced in wood and tiles. These were the first undisturbed royal Western Han tombs ever discovered. Inside, the dead rested in lacquered and inlaid coffins. Critic and author Bamber Gascoigne describes what the archaeologists found:

> Each tomb consisted of several interconnecting chambers, with even a room for bathing, and they contained in all nearly 3000 objects—bronze, gold, jade, silver, pottery, silk and lacquerware. Each entire treasure house had been sealed with a solid iron wall, made by pouring molten metal between two layers of bricks.

> The most magnificent of the contents were the two jade suits. . . . Each was composed of more than 2000 separate squares of jade, every one of them with four holes drilled in the corners to attach it with gold wire to its neighbours. The work involved was colossal, given the extraordinary hardness of jade, and in terms of their

A jade funeral suit excavated from the tomb of Prince Liu Sheng of the Han dynasty.

purpose these expensive garments were a complete failure. It was considered that jade contained a magical property of preserving bodies. In fact its very hardness and weight seem to have had precisely the opposite effect. In various other tombs bodies have been found which, although treated far more simply, have survived in an almost mummified state. Of Liu Sheng and his wife Tou [Dou] Wan there remained, within their beautiful suits, nothing but dust.[1]

Archaeologists knew from ancient texts that such jade burial suits existed. They also knew that the Han had used such suits only for the highest-ranking nobles and that the rank of the deceased determined whether the suit was sewn with gold, silver, or bronze thread. The two suits unearthed at Mancheng were the earliest and most complete examples of such suits discovered at that point in time. Experts estimate that it would have taken ten years to make a jade suit like the one that served as Liu Sheng's shroud.

Liu Sheng died in 113 B.C. He and Dou Wan lived and died in the era before the Christian one when a dynasty known as the Han ruled China. Liu Sheng was a member of the Han nobility, the ninth son of the emperor Jingdi, and the ruler in his own right of the ancient Chinese kingdom of Zhongshan. His tomb is ranked as one of the top ten archaeological discoveries in China during the twentieth century.

Among the grave goods in the tombs of Liu Sheng and Dou Wan were items made of bronze, such as Liu Sheng's headrest, the exceptional quality of which verified that the deceased were of high rank. There were also gold and silver acupuncture needles, bronze daggers, some vessels inlaid with gold and silver thread, and some undecorated pieces typical of the period from the second century B.C. on. In the south side-chamber were a half-dozen chariots. All of these artifacts provided valuable information about the movement of objects, gifts received from other courts, ancient pieces passed down as legacies, and exotic objects brought back from abroad. They also served as an indication of the rank and lifestyles of the tombs' occupants.

Experts estimate that the Han constructed more than ten thousand tombs for emperors, nobles, and officials. Liu Sheng's tomb is just one of more than forty Han mausoleums that have been unearthed in recent decades. The reason so many still exist today is that the Han built them mostly of brick and stone. They then placed them deep in the earth so they would not rot, be destroyed, or become easy prey for thieves and looters. Many of the objects found in Liu Sheng's tomb, such as the two sets of jade suits sewn with gold thread and the delicate gold-inlaid furnace, are thought to be unique. The jade suits, which were supposed to protect the body so it could reach the paradise of the immortals, provided evidence of a phenomenon mentioned in ancient texts: the quest for immortality.

The Han, like many other ancient cultures, buried with their dead all kinds of items they thought could be used in the afterlife. As a result, tombs, pits, and their surrounding areas supply the greatest part of what is known about Han China. According to experts, funerary objects are especially valuable because they reproduce the life of the Han. In 2000, for example, Chinese archaeologists found in the tomb of a Han king a toilet complete with running water, a stone seat, and an armrest. They reported that the "top-grade stool" was the "earliest of its kind ever discovered in the world, meaning that the Chinese used the world's earliest water closet, which is quite like what we are using today."[2] Collectively, the tombs contain a great number of diverse historical and cultural relics, each of which helps piece together the puzzle of what happened during the Han dynasty and what life was like for the Han people.

The First Successful Dynasty

That the tombs contain objects archaeologists consider unique is not surprising, for the Han dynasty itself was unique. The fifth dynasty to rule China, the Han were in power almost continuously from 206 B.C. to approximately A.D. 220—more than four hundred years—the longest lasting dynasty of the recorded imperial age. Many historians believe that China went through its first great development during the Han dynasty. And most would agree with historian Michael Loewe's contention that

> The Han period marks the first lengthy operation of imperial unity, in the sense of the continuity of a single dynastic house. It was a time for cultural dissemination and uniformity, in which many aspects of Chinese genius were fostered and brought to a flowering. Later dynasties were to look back to the Han period as a time of Chinese strength and resolution; and as the Han was regarded as the first of China's successful dynasties, the political forms and intellectual conclusions of the time have exercised a formative influence on succeeding dynasties.[3]

Loewe and other historians have not based their conclusions about the importance of the Han entirely on tombs and funerary objects. In 2001, Chinese farmers digging a pit on a hill near their village in central China found a pottery jar filled with more than ten thousand bronze coins from the Han dynasty. The coins proved to be from mintages covering more than 350 years of Han rule. According to the archaeologists who cleaned and sorted them, the an-

A collection of terra-cotta musicians, dancers, and servants. Such clay figurines feature prominently among the funerary objects in Han tombs.

cient coins offer a great deal of insight into the politics, economy, and culture of the Han dynasty.

The writings and records of Han officials and historians also have contributed to modern-day knowledge of the Han, their way of life, their achievements, and the beliefs and events that shaped their society. Han officials meticulously recorded the "statistics" of their times, while Han historians chronicled events, beliefs, and government actions, as well as the lives of those they considered important.

The Han defined the Chinese national identity and placed China in the forefront of the world's ancient civilized countries. Theirs was a period of power and glory, orderly growth, and awe-inspiring accomplishment during which China's borders were expanded and a stable government was established. Building on a foundation of institutions and traditions initiated by earlier dynasties, the Han gave credence to a dynastic form of government that would continue in both theory and practice into the 1900s— a government made up of a single ruler, government officials, a system of laws, and an official ideology. In recognition of this and of the Han's other great achievements, modern-day governments use the term *Han* to differentiate the ethnic Chinese from other racial and cultural groups within China.

CHAPTER ONE

BUILDING FOUNDATIONS: BEFORE THE HAN

Different groups of people think of their history in different ways. The Chinese think of their history politically and in terms of the more than twenty-five dynasties that claimed authority over part or all of their territory over a period of more than two thousand years. In power from 206 B.C. to A.D. 9 and then again from A.D. 25 to A.D. 220, the Han were the fifth of those twenty-five dynasties. Before them came the Xia, the Shang, the Zhou, and the Qin, each of which influenced the Han in particular and enriched Chinese culture and society in general.

According to Chinese legend, dynastic rule began in about 2000 B.C. when the Xia dynasty was founded by an ancient engineer named Yü. Chinese folklore, legends, and histories across the ages relate stories about Yü's exploits and his devotion to duty. This trait would serve as a constant example to Han officials. Until the twentieth century, however, there was no supporting archaeological evidence that Yü or the Xia dynasty actually existed. Scientific excavations in 1928 revealed some information about the Xia but did not establish what was myth and what was reality. Not until 1959, when excavators at Erlitous in the city of Yanshi uncovered what is believed to be a capital of the Xia dynasty, did archaeologists find any real

evidence of the dynasty's existence. Radiocarbon dates from the site showed that the Xia existed from 2100 B.C. to 1800 B.C. Later still, in the 1960s and 1970s, archaeologists uncovered urban sites, bronze implements, and tombs that made experts believe that the Xia civilization existed in the same locations cited in ancient Chinese historical texts.

The Shang

Until the 1920s, historians also thought that the second Chinese dynasty—the Shang—might not have really existed. But then inscriptions were found at an excavation on the Yellow River near the modern town of Anyang that indicated that the site was Ta Shang, the last capital of the Shang dynasty. Most of what is known about the Shang comes from this site. According to archaeologist Kwang-chih Chang,

> The bulk of ancient writings were unquestionably written on bamboo or wooden tablets or on silk fabrics. . . . Unfortunately, as far as being physically handed down to posterity goes, bamboo and silk were very poor materials for the purpose. . . . We do know that in the royal court of the Shang dynasty . . . there were

A bronze cooking vessel known as a fandang, from the Shang dynasty.

archivists and scribes who recorded important events of the state. With brush and ink, they transcribed characters onto slips of bamboo or wood and bound them together into book form (the so-called ts'e). . . .

As to what is engraved on metal and stone and what is cut on vessels, we have from the Shang . . . a large number of inscriptions on bronze ritual vessels, musical instruments, weapons, and a few other objects.[4]

The inscriptions the excavators uncovered at the site were the first written records recovered from an early Chinese people and proved that the Shang were not just myth or legend.

Historians believe the Shang dynasty was founded around 1700 B.C. by a rebel leader who overthrew the Xia ruler. Objects unearthed by archaeologists indicate that the Shang made their tools of stone and their weapons, ritual vessels, and chariot fittings of bronze. Archaeological evidence indicates that bronze making was a major industry during the Shang period. Many ritual bronzes were engraved with records of the military exploits of rulers, making them very valuable for historical research. Because of the quality of casting, intricate designs, uniqueness, and richness of Shang bronzes unearthed at Anyang and other Shang sites, many experts consider the Shang the most advanced bronze-working civilization in the world. Even the bronze objects crafted later by the Han did not equal the quality of those of the Shang.

The Shang ruler and his court believed in divination, the art or act of predicting the future. Shang mystics known as soothsayers or diviners performed a special ceremony to answer questions and foretell the future. The ceremony centered on animal bones and tortoise shells, which came to be known as oracle bones. Holes were drilled in the bones and shells, a question was asked, and then the bones and shells were placed into a fire. The heat of the fire caused cracks to appear, which the soothsayers interpreted to predict the outcome of an event. The soothsayers carved the date, questions, and the interpretations on the bones to refer to in the future.

At Xiaotun, the site of the remains of the Shang capital, archaeologists have unearthed more than 100,000 oracle bones carved with words. These inscriptions, with their vocabulary of more than four thousand characters, are the earliest known version of the writing system still in use in China today. Only about seven hundred of the characters have been deciphered so far.

Both the writing and the belief in divination passed from the Shang to other dynasties, including the Han. Historical documents and artifacts found in Han tombs have shown that Han of all classes practiced divination, using as their instruments not only oracle bones but also the stalks of the yarrow plant, cloud formations in the sky, the winds, and comets and other astrological events.

The Zhou: The Sons of Heaven

About 1000 B.C., the Shang were overthrown by the Zhou, who shared the language and culture of the Shang. Although

An oracle bone with inscriptions unearthed at Xiaotun, the Shang capital.

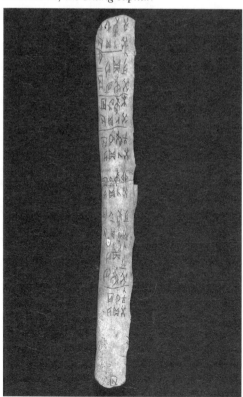

the Zhou extended Shang culture throughout much of China north of the Yangtze River, they did not rule all of China. At the time, Chinese territory was made up of a number of principalities, of which the Zhou territory was one. Because the Zhou principality was in the midst of the other principalities, it was known as the Middle Kingdom. Over time, the term *Middle Kingdom* broadened until it came to mean center of the world.

According to a poem in the *Shijing*, the earliest known collection of Chinese poems, the foundation of the Zhou dynasty is owed to a duke named Tai Wang and his lady, who decided to make their home on the fertile plain of Chou (Zhou) and ordered that houses be built there. The poem describes how the duke "drew the boundaries of big plots and little, opened up the ground, and counted the acres from west to east." After that, writes the poet,

> He [the duke] summoned his Master
>   of Works,
> Then he summoned his Master of Lands
> And made them build houses. . . .
> They tiled in the earth with a rattling,
> They pounded it with a dull thud,
> They beat the walls with a loud clang,
> They pared and chiseled them with
>   a faint p'ing, p'ing;
> The hundred cubits all rose. . . .
> They raised the outer gate;
> The outer gate soared high.
> They raised the inner gate;
> The inner gate was very strong.
> They raised the great earth-mound,
> Whence excursions of war might start.[5]

Zhou rulers believed they were *Tien Tzu* (sons of Heaven) directly descended from

A TREASURE OF ANCIENT POETRY: *SHIJING*

Shijing, also known as *The Book of Songs* and *The Book of Odes,* is the earliest known collection of Chinese poems. The anthology, which includes more than three hundred Zhou dynasty poems, was given the name *Shijing* by Confucians of the Han dynasty and was passed down to the present time by a Han dynasty Confucian scholar named Mao Heng. In his honor, the work is also called *Maoshi,* or *Mao Poems.*

Shijing is the source of Chinese verse and the origin of Chinese epic literature. It includes history poems, satirical poems, narrative poems, love songs, odes, seasonal songs, and work songs. The work covers all aspects of the society of the Zhou dynasty, from work, to love, to war, to customs and marriage, to sacrifices and feasts. Some historians and academicians dedicated to the study of Chinese culture consider *Shijing* the most valuable and important material in the study of the Chinese language from the eleventh century to the sixth century B.C.

Tien, or Heaven. Heaven, they said, had chosen them to rule because they were virtuous and worthy. If they were overthrown, it proved that they had done something not virtuous and had lost the mandate to rule (the "Mandate of Heaven") or that someone more virtuous had taken over. In this way, the Zhou explained and justified the fall of the Xia and the Shang dynasties. Later, the Han would use the same rationale to justify their overthrow of the Qin dynasty.

Zhou kings set up an agricultural system in which nobles owned the land and peasants worked it. City-states came into being, each made up of a walled town and the surrounding countryside. The Zhou rulers appointed their relatives to govern these city-states and gave them total authority over their own land as long as they remained loyal to the king.

Emerging Philosophies

Three historically important philosophies, all of which were to influence the Han, appeared during Zhou rule—Daoism, Legalism, and Confucianism. All three had a greater influence on later dynasties than they did on the Zhou. Daoism, which stressed a return to nature and quiet simplicity as a way of life, did not really take shape until late in the first period of Han rule and did not really flourish until the second period of Han rule. Legalism, which stressed power and held law as the supreme authority, became very important under the Qin, the dynasty overthrown by the Han. However, neither Daoism nor Legalism had as much influence on China as Confucianism, the moral, social, and ethical teachings of the philosopher born during the Zhou dynasty known as Confucius, or "Master K'ung." Long after his death, Confucius became the dominant Chinese philosopher both morally and politically, and his philosophy grew into one of the traditional religions of the Han Chinese.

Born in 551 B.C. in the principality of Lu in the modern-day Chinese province of Shandong, Confucius came from a family that was noble but poor. His parents died young, leaving him to make his own future. Wanting to investigate what factors contributed to good government and the way society worked, Confucius left home to visit neighboring courts. Upon his return, he founded a school of wisdom. Although Confucius is highly quoted and has many followers even today, he did not leave any written work. According to French historian and Chinese studies expert René Grousset,

> Confucius' aphorisms [adages] and those of his conversations that we possess have reached us only by way of an amended edition of some five hundred years after his death. . . .
>
> In so far as we are able to follow the course of his thought, it would seem that Confucius in no way sought after innovations. After the fashion of the old schools of the scribes with which he was connected, his teaching appears as a commentary on the tradition of the ancients. One finds in him again the respect proper to Heaven, that is to the cosmic order . . . which . . . in Confucius generally

means the right (i.e. the ancient) way of government.

Like all the sages of his school, Confucius preaches filial piety and piety towards . . . the cult of ancestors. Despite this traditionalism, . . . what he appears to have prized above all was purity of intention and sincerity of heart. His doctrine appears to be essentially one of action, his teaching an active morality. It is as a director

A bronze statue of Confucius stands in Chatham Square in New York's Chinatown.

of conscience that he appears to have "won his prestige."[6]

The potential and power of Confucius's teachings were not fully realized until the Han dynasty. Under the Han, his teachings became the guiding philosophy of the Chinese empire and remained so until well into the twentieth century A.D.

The "Tiger of Qin" Unites China for the First Time

Around 221 B.C., the Zhou lost the Mandate of Heaven to Zhao Zheng, the "Tiger of Qin," ruler of the northwestern state of Qin. Known as the "land within the passes," Qin territory was a mountain-ringed fortress next to the northern territory that came to be known as Mongolia. The Qin were fierce swordsmen and crossbow warriors whom most other Chinese considered no better than savages.

Zhao Zheng pronounced himself *huangdi*, First August Sovereign, a title previously used only for gods and mythological figures. (*Huang* meant radiant, illustrious, or glorious, and *di* was what the Shang had called their highest spirit kings.) He became known as First Emperor—Shi huangdi. Like the Zhou rulers before him and the Han rulers after him, Shi huangdi considered himself the "Son of Heaven" and believed he had a divine right to rule. From that time on until 1911, *huangdi* remained the highest title of rulers of China.

An ambitious and ruthless tyrant, Shi huangdi set out to do away with warlords and other kingdoms and unify all of China under Qin rule. The Han would continue and improve upon this Qin tradition of centralization of power. Like Shi huangdi and his chief minister, Li Si, some members of the Han dynasty also believed in the doctrine of Legalism, which advocated strict laws and severe punishment. Legalists believed government should be a science, which it would not be unless governors refused to be deceived by such moral and impractical disruptions as humanity and tradition. Shi huangdi made Legalism the Qin's official government doctrine and established a harsh penal code under which many Chinese were sentenced to hard labor or worse. A person judged guilty of a serious offense was beheaded, chopped in half at the waist, or boiled to death in a huge cauldron.

Together, Li Si and Shi huangdi attained their goal of a strong central government with a carefully formulated and strictly enforced code of law. In the process, they forever changed the way China was ruled. First they broke up the existing feudal structure of local kings and noble families. Then they established thirty-six regional provinces, each divided into prefectures that, in turn, were divided into counties. The counties were further divided into districts and hamlets. Officials accountable to the emperor's top deputies were appointed to govern the counties. In addition to the top deputies there was a nine-minister cabinet, with each minister in charge of a different area, such as justice, ceremonial rites, or the treasury.

With this structure, which the Han later took as their own and enhanced, the Qin united all of China under one central government headed by the emperor. At the same time, Shi huangdi unified Chinese culture by standardizing the legal code, the characters used in Chinese writing, weights and measures, coinage, and even the size of cart wheels. He also introduced coins called

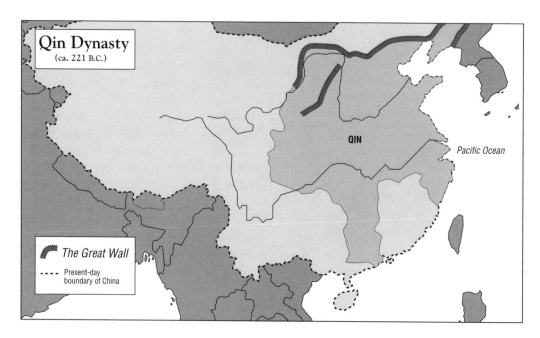

Qin Dynasty
(ca. 221 B.C.)

QIN

Pacific Ocean

The Great Wall

- - - - Present-day
boundary of China

cash used later by the Han and other dynasties. According to historian Ray Huang,

> If a single development in Chinese history sets it far apart from other civilizations in the world, it is the imperial unification of the Qin in 221 B.C. The political maturity that this feat required . . . fixed the pattern of centralization that was to be followed for millenniums. The record is startling. . . .

> China's imperial unification under the Qin is a major milestone in world history. No parallel to the gigantic spiral movement toward it . . . has occurred elsewhere in the world.[7]

The Qin Expand the Empire and Build a Wall

Shi huangdi sent out armies to invade and conquer neighboring peoples. To the north-

west, the Qin defeated the Huns, nomadic horse-mounted warriors they knew as Xiongnu. To the northeast, the Qin convinced the prince who ruled Korea to acknowledge Qin authority. To the south, Qin armies bested the Yueh tribes and eventually moved into what became Vietnam.

Having expanded their territory, the Qin set out to strengthen their defenses against barbarian raiders to the north. In the past, walls had been built in the northern provinces to deter invaders. The Qin joined all these walls into one large wall by filling in the gaps and reinforcing the existing structures. In addition, the Qin erected forty-foot towers every few hundred yards in which to station their archers. The entire project was a massive undertaking. According to *Ancient China* author Brian Williams,

> The result was one continuous wall that ran from the Yellow Sea to the

east to the semidesert Turkestan region in the west. More than one million workers took part in the project, which took seven years to complete. So many workers died in the process that the wall came to be known as the longest cemetery in the world.

The project was run like an army. Supply camps were set up to ferry food and materials to the mountains and deserts of the northern frontier. Soldiers were posted to the vast building site to fight off bandits and to stop workers from running away. Thousands of peasants were marched from their fields to work on the Wall. Many of them never returned home. One consequence of this was that crops were neglected and many people went hungry.[8]

These building efforts eventually resulted in the Great Wall, which the Han later restored and extended an additional three hundred miles. Added on to and restored by a number of dynasties, the wall still stands today as a testimony to the skill and enduring legacy of China's ancient dynasties.

Erasing History

Shi huangdi took pride in his victories and boasted freely of how great he was. He traveled his empire and at some places he visited had tributes to himself inscribed on stone. The following inscription is just one of many:

> When the sage of Qin took charge of his state, he first determined punishments and names, and clearly set forth the ancient regulations. He was the first to standardize the system of

The serpentine Great Wall was designed to repel barbarian raiders from the north.

LI SI ADVISES THE EMPEROR

About a year after the Qin chief minister Li Si burned the books written by thinkers of earlier dynasties, Shi huangdi ordered the execution of more than four hundred scholars because he suspected them of conspiring against him. In his work *Shiji*, written long after the burning and the execution, Han historian Sima Qian writes that Li Si defended these harsh acts as necessary to maintain order and respect for authority. In this translation from *Shiji* in William Theodore de Bary and Irene Bloom's *Sources of Chinese Tradition: From Earliest Times to 1600*, Li Si warns the emperor about scholars speaking out against the empire.

> These independent schools, joining with each other, criticize the codes of laws and instructions. Hearing of the promulgation of a decree, they criticize it, each from the standpoint of his own school. At home they disapprove of it in their hearts; going out they criticize it in the thoroughfare. They seek a reputation by discrediting their sovereign; they appear superior by expressing contrary views; and they lead the lowly multitude in the spreading of slander. If such license is not prohibited, the sovereign power will decline above and partisan factions will form below. It would be well to prohibit this.

laws, examine and demarcate duties and responsibilities, so as to establish unchanging practices. The August Emperor has unified the universe, and he pays attention to all of the myriad concerns, and both near and far are made pure. . . . His great rule cleanses morality, and all under Heaven come under his influence, and are the beneficiaries of his bountiful regime. Everyone honors the rules, and earnestly strives in harmony and tranquility, and nobody does not obey orders. . . . Posterity will accept the law with respect, and perpetual government will have no ending.[9]

Not all Chinese, however, agreed with this assessment of Shi huangdi's attributes, accomplishments, empire, or government. Many scholars, for example, opposed the doctrine of Legalism advocated by Shi huangdi and Li Si. Angered by the attitude of the scholars, Li Si began a campaign to rid the empire of intellectual, ethical writings, which he believed represented past thinking that contradicted that of the Qin. According to *Shiji*, written by Sima Qian, grand historian of the Han dynasty, Li Si made this suggestion to Shi huangdi:

> Your servant suggests that all books in the imperial archives, save the memoirs of Qin, be burned. All persons in the empire, except members of the Academy of Learned Scholars, in possession of the Classic of Odes, the Classic of Documents, and discourses of the hundred philosophers should take them to the local governors and have them indiscriminately burned. Those who dare to talk to each other about the Odes and Documents should be executed and their bodies exposed in the marketplace. Anyone referring to the past to criticize the present should, together with all members of his family, be put to death. Officials who fail to report cases that have come under their attention are equally guilty. After thirty days from the time of issuing the decree, those who have not destroyed their books are to be branded and sent to build the Great Wall. Books not to be destroyed will be those on medicine and pharmacy, divination by the turtle and milfoil, and agriculture and arboriculture. People wishing to pursue learning should take the officials as their teachers.[10]

In 213 B.C., history, philosophy, and poetry books written before the Qin took power were burned. Modern-day authors Caroline Blunden and Mark Elvin explain the impact of this act: "The destruction of books and the compulsory reform of the script meant that almost all the old writings were imperfectly transmitted to later ages, or lost altogether."[11]

Qin rule did not last long after the First Emperor died in 210 B.C. The son who took his place was weak. Neither he nor his ministers, who often intrigued against him, could put down the peasant uprisings that kept erupting. The dynasty fell apart as revolution broke out. Four years of war followed during which two strong leaders, Xiangyu and Liu Bang, fought to dominate the country. Finally, Liu Bang won out and established a new dynasty—the Han.

FOUR HUNDRED YEARS OF POWER

When Liu Bang, once a minor Qin official, declared himself emperor of the Han in 202 B.C. and took the imperial title Gaozu, "high progenitor," he initiated a dynasty that would revolutionize China over a period of more than four hundred years. Liu Bang ruled in the period of the Western Han dynasty (so named because the dynasty's capital city was Chang'an in the western part of China). The time of the Western Han is also referred to as the Former Han dynasty and the Earlier Han dynasty, and it encompassed a series of emperors that ruled until A.D. 9.

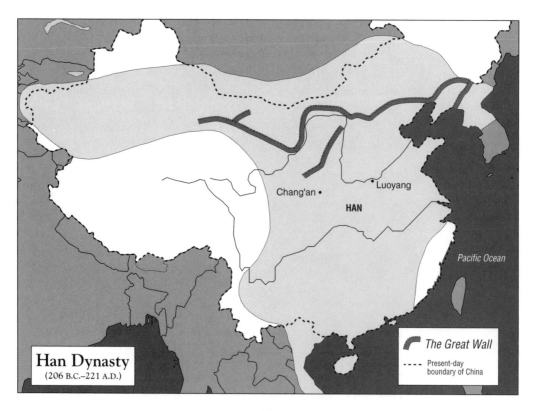

Chang'an •   • Luoyang

HAN

Pacific Ocean

Han Dynasty
(206 B.C.–221 A.D.)

The Great Wall

- - - - Present-day boundary of China

WUDI: THE MIGHTY ONE

The distinguished Han poet Sima Xiangru, who died in 117 B.C., dedicated one of his poems, "The Mighty One," to the Han emperor Wudi, during whose reign Sima lived. This translation by Barton Watson of two verses of Sima Xiangru's long ode is taken from John Minford and Joseph S.M. Lau's anthology *Classical Chinese Literature*.

> In this world there lives a Mighty One
> Who dwells in the Middle Continent [China].
> Though his mansion stretches ten thousand miles,
> He is not content to remain in it a moment
> But, saddened by the sordid press of the vulgar world,
> Nimbly takes his way aloft and soars far away. . . .
> His elephant-carved chariot is drawn by winged dragons,
> With red serpents and green lizards writhing at their sides. . . .
> They careen wildly across the sky.
>
> He orders the Emperors of the Five Directions to be his guides. . . .
> His cortege boasts ten thousand carriages,
> In endless massive ranks his retinue advances; . . .
> With his attendant carriages, he gallops the long road downward,
> Racing through the mists and off into the distance.
> He presses beyond the borders of the narrow universe. . . .
> Beneath him in the vastness, the earth has disappeared;
> Above his head the heavens vanish in endless space.
> Gazing about, his eyes swim and grow sightless;
> His ears are deafened and discern no sound.
> Riding upon the Void, he mounts on high,
> Above the world of men, companionless, to dwell alone.

According to Grand Historian Sima Qian, "When Sima Xiangru presented his ode in praise of the Mighty One, the emperor was overcome with delight, declaring that it made him feel as though he were already soaring effortlessly over the clouds and filled him with a longing to wander about the earth and the heavens."

By 140 B.C. Liu Bang and three other emperors had come and gone. That year, however, a fifteen-year-old boy became the fifth Han emperor. He was known as Wudi, the "warrior emperor" or the "martial emperor," and he is recognized as one of the most successful emperors in the history of China. Historians believe his fifty-four-year reign, the high point of the Han period, launched a new era in China's history. It was a reign marked by military expansion, political centralization, and cultural achievements.

Wudi had been emperor for about twenty years when he made Confucianism the official moral and political doctrine around which all politics, society, and culture revolved. He successfully used it to promote cultural unity. Under Wudi's rule, the Han developed a basic system of strong central government based on Confucianism and run by a salaried bureaucracy appointed on the basis of a civil service system. The Confucian emphasis on learning, harmony, moderation, tolerance, courtesy, and respect for the past dominated everything the Han did.

Expanding the Empire

During the many centuries of Han rule, China grew as large and as powerful as the Roman Empire, reaching and defining the borders it would maintain almost continuously well into modern times. The Han persistently pushed China's frontiers outward. In the process, they opened their once-isolated empire to trade, people, and new ideas. The greatest expansion took place during the reign of Wudi, when the empire was stable and the imperial treasury was full from conquests, the improved governance, and the rise of trade. Wudi's armies extended Han political and cultural influence west to Xinjiang and Central Asia, north to Manchuria and Korea, and south to Yunnan, Hainan Island, and Vietnam.

Wudi created a large, well-equipped, better-trained military with strong leaders and sent his armies out to seek victory over the barbarians outside of the Great Wall the Qin had built. Archaeologists have discovered clay replicas of Han foot soldiers and cavalry in tombs belonging to the Han military officer. The tomb of General Chou Pou near Xianyang in Shanxi province, excavated in 1956, for example, yielded more than six hundred mounted earthenware cavalry soldiers, giving a small yet impressive indication of the massive armies these men must have commanded.

Historians believed that the military strength of the Han was due to their supportive bureaucratic structure and their command of advanced weaponry. The Han invented the crossbow, which both cavalry and foot soldiers used to great effect. The fact that the weapon could be precocked gave the soldier greater control over the aiming and discharge of the bolt, the special arrow devised for the crossbow. In addition, the force built up in the mechanically wound bowstring meant that a released bolt had the power to pierce many different forms of armor.

Wudi did more than arm his soldiers with crossbows. He changed the military in other ways as well. As historian John Hood explains,

He armed his new military with iron and steel swords, plate or scale mail and crossbows. Wudi's armies were also increasingly composed of highly skilled, experienced mercenaries [paid soldiers], many on horseback, rather

THE CELESTIAL HORSES OF FERGHANA

In October 1969, a general's tomb from the second century A.D., discovered near Wu-wei in China's Gansu province, yielded bronze statuettes of horses. Among the statuettes was the famous "Flying Horse," its head and tail raised high in a proud gallop, thought to be one of the finest known works of Han art. Art historians and connoisseurs consider it the best representation of the living Celestial Horse known today.

The bronze statuette is a miniature of the horses that the Han imported from Ferghana, in modern-day Kyrgyzstan. In the second century B.C., Zhang Qian, on expedition at the request of his emperor, came upon the kingdom of Ferghana, where he saw "mighty horses that sweat blood." When he told Emperor Wudi about these horses, Wudi was determined to bring the "Heavenly Horses," or "Celestial Horses," to his court. When all else failed, Wudi sent his armies to Ferghana to convince the rulers of the kingdom to part with the horses. After two years of battle, Wudi's armies returned home with many celestial horses, three thousand stallions and mares, and the promise that every year Wudi would receive two celestial horses.

The Chinese believed that Celestial Horses descended from supernatural horses and had been granted special powers by Heaven. Larger, stronger, faster, and with greater endurance than any horses known to the Han, the Celestial Horse did much to improve the dynasty's military strength. According to legend, the horses could run the length of the empire and back in one day. The Chinese compared the horses' strength and spirit to that of dragons, and they soon became status symbols for the wealthy and offi- cials. Just having horses was a sign of wealth because one horse alone consumed as much grain as an ordinary family of six people. Earthenware and bronze sculptures, small and large, of the horses became important funerary objects in the tombs of Han aristocrats.

The exquisite bronze "Flying Horse" excavated at Wu-wei.

than the poorly trained conscripted footmen [unpaid peasants] of earlier Han and Qin armies. Wudi's armies benefited from the leadership of valorous and talented generals. They enjoyed good logistics. And they were always closely followed in victory by Chinese officials, settlers and artisans, who imposed cultural hegemony [control].[12]

Han armies pushed northward, penetrating deep into the Xiongnu territory in what is now Mongolia. Although they never totally defeated the Xiongnu, their victories far outweighed their losses. They took back territory that had been part of the empire in the past but lost in recent years, such as part of Annam (Vietnam). They also conquered parts of Manchuria and Korea and established a colony in Korea that for the next four hundred years remained a Chinese outpost.

Extending the Great Wall

The Han valued their territory—new and old—and wanted to keep it safe from outside invaders. In an effort to do this, they restored the crumbling Qin Great Wall and then extended it for three hundred more miles across the sands of the Gobi Desert, expanding China farther west than ever before. Building a wall in the Gobi Desert was no easy task. The workers began by laying a bed of red willow reeds and twigs at the

A team of laborers works to expand the Great Wall.

THE HISTORIES OF SIMA QIAN AND BAN GU

Much of what is known about early dynastic Chinese history comes from the writings of two Han historians—Sima Qian and Ban Gu. Both described the history of the Han in great detail. And in keeping with the style of their times, both wrote histories intended more to preserve traditions than to reveal underlying truths.

Sima Qian (145–86 B.C.) trained as an astronomer and a historian and was a palace scribe at the court of Emperor Wudi. The idea to write a history book began with his father, who had served as Grand Historian, a position he passed on to his son. As grand historian, Sima Qian had to establish and maintain the royal calendar and compose a record of the principal events of the reign. His *Records of the Historian (Shiji)* established a pattern for future Chinese historical writing. His belief that history should teach lessons and reveal the values of the society being remembered is reflected in his work, which chronicles the story of the Chinese world from its beginnings to Sima Qian's own times. The work is divided into five separate sections—basic annals, a chronology, a description of the government, a long biographical section in which the lives and deeds of great men were recorded, and an autobiographical section.

Ban Gu (A.D. 32–92) was a historian for the Eastern Han and Xin dynasties, a scholar familiar with the teachings of all schools of thought, and a writer of many histories, poetry, and prose. His father, an official during the early years of the Eastern Han dynasty, wrote a sixty-five-chapter supplement to Sima Qian's *Shiji*. On his deathbed, Ban Gu's father asked him to finish the history he had started of the Former (Western) Han. Using the historical materials his father had collected, Ban Gu compiled *The History of the Former Han (Hanshu)*, also known as *Book of Han*, which covers the reign of twelve Han emperors, from Gaozu to Pingdi—almost three hundred years of Han history. Ban Gu died before he could complete the work, leaving his younger sister, Ban Zhao, a scholar and writer in her own right, to complete the work. The completed *Book of Han* is both a chronicle of events and a compendium of the knowledge of the age, including such subjects as mathematics and astronomy. It was the first of China's twenty-five dynastic histories (unlike *Shiji*, which was the first universal history of China) and the only history to include a chapter specifically devoted to geography.

bottom of a wooden frame and then filling the frame with a mixture of water, dirt, and fine gravel, which they packed down tightly enough to make the mixture solid. When the mixture was dry all the way through, they took away the wooden frame, leaving behind a solid slab of packed earth.

Han laborers built up new channels and barriers all along the Wall, as well as beacon towers every fifteen to thirty miles. Historical records and inscribed bamboo slips have been found inside some of the beacon towers. These artifacts indicated that a chief function of the towers was to transmit military information, which made the wall vital for communications as well as defense. According to one modern-day source,

> Along its ramparts messages could be sent at amazing speeds from one end of the empire to the other. . . . From the [beacon towers] the Han troops used smoke by day and torches by night to send messages along the length of the wall. They burnt wood and straw mixed with wolf dung, which produced rich black columns of smoke. . . . One column of smoke indicated an impending attack by a force of less than 500. Two columns indicated an attack by a force less than 3000 and four columns indicated an attack by a force of up to 10,000.[13]

The Han, like the Qin before them, drafted a lot of workers to construct sections of the Great Wall. Many of those workers never returned home. In this excerpt from the poem "I Watered My Horse at the Long Wall Caves" by the Eastern Han poet Ch'en Lin, a laborer drafted to work on the wall bemoans the fate of the laborers and their wives:

I watered my horse at the Long Wall caves,
Water so cold it hurt his bones;
I went and spoke to the Long Wall boss:
"We're soldiers from T'ai-yüan—will you keep us here forever?"
"Public works go according to schedule—
swing your hammer, pitch your voice in with the rest!"
A man'd be better off to die in battle
Than eat his heart out building the Long Wall!
The Long Wall—how it winds and winds,
Winds and winds three thousand li;
Here on the border, so many strong boys;
In the houses back home, so many widows and wives.[14]

Relics of the original Han constructions can still be found today in places where the Great Wall crests high mountains. In 2001 a new section of wall was uncovered. According to historical records, more than 600, 000 laborers were mobilized to build the portion of the wall from Dunhuang to Yanze, the present site of Lop Nur, where the new section of wall was uncovered. Frescoes found in the Buddhist cave temples of the Dunhuang Grottoes in Central Asia west of modern-day Xian depict the massive construction project.

The Silk Road

A mural found in one of the caves of the Mogao Grottoes in the oasis town of Dunhuang shows a man leaving on a journey bidding farewell to the Emperor Wudi. The man is Zhang Qian, a commander of the guards at the gates of the Han imperial palace. In

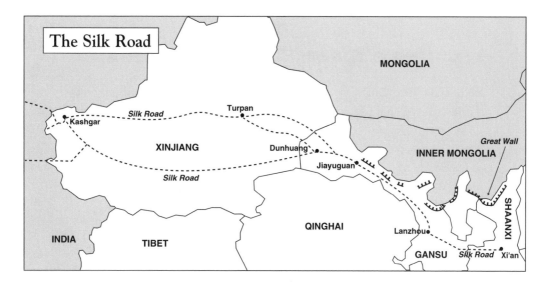

138 B.C. he and a band of about one hundred Chinese set out to the western steppes to find and form an alliance with a tribe called Yuezhi. The journey took Zhang Qian northeast of Iran to the ancient country of Bactria in a region that is now part of Afghanistan, Uzbekistan, and Tajikistan. Thirteen years passed before he and the one remaining survivor from his original band returned home. Upon their return, they brought the emperor animal and plant specimens, including cultivated grapes, which the Chinese had never seen before. The travelers intrigued the emperor with stories about their many adventures, the wealthy lands, and the strange people they had seen. Historians believe these were the first reliable descriptions of Central Asia received by the Chinese.

Zhang's journey and his report to the emperor led to the establishment of the Silk Road, a major trade corridor across western China and Central Asia that linked China and the West. The trade route took its name from the fine silk cloth that was China's most successful article of trade. By the time of the Han, the Chinese silk industry had highly developed techniques and was producing a number of elegant silk fabrics and garments. The beauty and quality of Han silk is evidenced in the silk fabrics and paintings uncovered from 1972 to 1974 in the Mawangdui Western Han tombs of the Marquis Dai and his wife and son.

The opening of the eastern half of the Silk Road helped open new worlds to China because, along with trade goods, information and knowledge was passed among cultures in the East and the West. Before long, trade caravans began to travel west to the Asian country of Parthia southeast of the Caspian Sea. They passed through the narrow strip of land between the mountains of Tibet and the northern deserts and on past the cities that came to be called Tashkent and Samarkand. Conversely, the roads taken by traders from Rome, Antioch, Baghdad, and Alexandria all passed through China's Great Wall. Caravans of camels carried the goods from one destination to the next. No other animal was equipped

CHINA'S FIRST FEMALE HISTORIAN

Ban Zhao, the daughter and younger sister of famous historians, was China's first female historian and the foremost female Confucian of the Han. She produced her most famous work, *Nü Jie (Lessons for a Woman)*, to show her daughters how a woman ought to behave. Her work so impressed Emperor He that he brought her to the palace to teach the empress and the imperial concubines the laws of moral conduct she had set down in *Nü Jie*. In her book *Pan Chao: Foremost Woman Scholar of China*, Nancy Lee Swann translates from *Nü Jie* Ban Zhao's lesson on humility.

On the third day after the birth of a girl the ancients observed three customs: first to place the baby below the bed; second to give her a potsherd [a piece of broken pottery] with which to play; and third to announce her birth to her ancestors by an offering. Now to lay the baby below the bed plainly indicated that she is lowly and weak, and should regard it as her primary duty to humble herself before others. To give her potsherds with which to play indubitably signified that she should practice labor and consider it her primary duty to be industrious. To announce her birth before her ancestors clearly meant that she ought to esteem as her primary duty the continuation of the observance of worship in the home.

These three ancient customs epitomize woman's ordinary way of life and the teachings of the traditional ceremonial rites and regulations.

to carry such heavy burdens through the dry, desolate lands that had to be crossed along the way. It was costly to transport the goods. It also was difficult. So, the caravans carried only luxury goods, such as gold, cinnamon, silk, and animal skins. The Chinese traded their goods for many different things— wine, spices, linen, horses, woolen goods, sesame, pomegranates, broad beans, and other food plants. At Parthia, the Chinese traded their goods to Iranian traders, who carried them to the Mediterranean.

The Han posted soldiers at a number of sites along the Silk Road to keep it safe from raids by warrior tribes. Along the route were independent states and ethnic groups. Over time, a number of these became Chinese subjects that paid tribute to the Han with goods and hostages, a common gesture of loyalty at the time.

The Silk Road and the wealth it brought the Han did not change the people's prevailing attitude toward merchants and traders, the men who carried out the transactions. In

Let a woman modestly yield to others; let her respect others; let her put others first, herself last. Should she do something good, let her not mention it; should she do something bad let her not deny it. Let her bear disgrace; let her even endure when others speak or do evil to her. Always let her seem to tremble and to fear. When a woman follows such maxims as these then she may be said to humble herself before others. Let a woman retire late to bed, but rise early to duties; let her not dread tasks by day or by night. Let her not refuse to perform domestic duties whether easy or difficult. That which must be done, let her finish completely, tidily, and systematically. When a woman follows such rules as these, then she may be said to be industrious.

Let a woman be correct in manner and upright in character in order to serve her husband. Let her live in purity and quietness of spirit, and attend to her own affairs. Let her love not gossip and silly laughter. Let her cleanse and purify and arrange in order the wine and the food for the offerings to the ancestors. When a woman observes such principles as these, then she may be said to continue ancestral worship.

No woman who observes these three fundamentals of life has ever had a bad reputation or has fallen into disgrace. If a woman fails to observe them, how can her name be honored; how can she but bring disgrace upon herself?

keeping with Confucian beliefs, the Han did not approve of engaging in trade. They viewed it as an unvirtuous striving for profit. And, like the Legalists of the Qin dynasty, they were suspicious of merchants, who they thought put their own interests ahead of those of the state and society. As far as the Han government was concerned, merchants were parasites who fed off farmers; in fact, the government barred merchants from holding office, owning land, or riding horses. The Han statesman Chao Cuo voiced these an-timerchant sentiments as early as 178 B.C. in his "Memorial on the Encouragement of Agriculture":

Among the traders and merchants . . . the larger ones hoard goods and exact 100 percent profit, while the smaller ones sit lined up in the markets selling their wares. Those who deal in luxury goods daily disport themselves in the cities and market towns; taking advantage of the ruler's wants, they are able to sell at double price. Thus though their men neither plow nor weed, though their women neither tend silkworms nor spin, yet their clothes are brightly patterned and colored, and they eat only choice grain and meat. They have none of the hardships of the farmer, yet their grain is ten to one hundredfold. With their wealth they may consort with nobles, and their power exceeds the authority of government officials. They use their profits to overthrow others. Over a thousand miles they wander at ease, their caps and cart covers filling the roads. They ride in fine carriages and drive fat horses, tread in silken shoes and trail white silk behind them. Thus it is that merchants encroach upon the farmers.[15]

Despite this unforgiving view of the business class, the fact was that trade was bringing wealth to the empire.

Death of a Dynasty

For all intents and purposes, the Han dynasty died two deaths. The Western Han

A pair of horsemen brandishing spears; bronze figures from the Eastern Han dynasty.

dynasty fell in A.D. 9 to a usurper named Wang Mang, who started a new dynasty, the Xin. Within less than twenty years, Wang Mang had lost the Mandate of Heaven—and his life—and a Han emperor once again ruled China. This new Han emperor established a new capital at Luoyang, beginning the Eastern, or later, Han dynasty. Then he set out to restore Han administrative power.

At first, the Eastern Han were as successful as the Western Han. They ruled for nearly two hundred years before their empire began to fall apart. Invasions by tribes outside the Great Wall had taken their toll, and so had weak administrations and rivalries among scholars, officials, imperial relatives, advisers, and generals. In A.D. 190 rebels burned down Luoyang, sending its inhabitants fleeing through the treacherous countryside to the old Western Han city of Chang'an.

Chang'an was not a haven for long, and many people soon fled from there as rebellion swept the land. Among those who fled around A.D. 195 was the Han poet Wang Can, whose poem "Seven Sorrows" describes his leaving. The wolves and tigers to which he refers in the poem are the rebel leaders getting ready to attack the city. The words "that falling spring" come from a song of sorrow written by a poet of the Zhou dynasty when his capital fell centuries ago.

The Western Capital in lawless
   disorder;
Wolves and tigers poised to prey on it:
I'll leave this middle realm, be gone,
Go far off to the tribes of Ching.
Parents and kin face me in sorrow,
Friends running after, pulling me back.
Out the gate I see
Only white bones that strew the
   broad plain.
A starving woman beside the road
Hugs her child, then lays it in the weeds,
Looks back at the sound of its wailing,
Wipes her tears and goes on alone:
"I don't even know when my own
   death will come—
how can I keep both of us alive?"
Whip up the horses, leave her behind—
I cannot bear to hear such words!
South I climb the crest of Pa-ling,
Turning my head to look back on
   Chang'an.
I know what he meant—that falling
   spring—
Sobbing racks my heart and bowels.[16]

The Han dynasty died its second—and final—death in A.D. 220 when the Eastern Han finally fell, setting off a 350-year period of disorder, confusion, and disunity. Often called China's Middle Ages, it was the longest period of turbulence in China's history.

CHAPTER THREE

THE ORDERLY UNDERPINNINGS OF SOCIETY

Like the Chinese who had come before them and those who came after them, the people of the Han dynasty had clearly defined beliefs and philosophies. Theirs was a well-ordered and disciplined life based on patterns dictated by the beliefs they valued. Above all, they believed that all aspects of life should reflect the order of the universe.

According to the Han, Earth was made up of nine continents, each separated from the other by water and each divided into nine regions, one of which was China. China was the Middle Kingdom, the core at the center surrounded by rings of territory occupied by loyal and subject peoples, with an outermost

ring made up of barbarians—people not Chinese. That the Chinese of the time thought they were superior to anyone outside of their empire is not surprising. Until the time of the Han, Chinese civilization had developed on its own, relatively isolated from other cultures by its physical and cultural geography. Other cultures were virtually unknown— and, when acknowledged, generally not understood—by the Han.

The Han believed strongly in cosmic forces. These forces, which had to be taken into account at all times, were interrelated and followed a very specific pattern. The forces were grouped in fives. There were

This finely modeled miniature house exhibits the respect for cosmic balance the Han incorporated into all structures.

Five Elements—water, fire, wood, metal, and earth. They corresponded to five directions—north, west, south, east, and center; five primary colors—black, white, red, blue-green, and yellow; and five sacred animals—bird, tiger, tortoise, dragon, and man. Each activity except earth corresponded to a particular season. Earth represented all seasons. Only one activity was supposed to be dominant at a given time, and each became more important in a fixed sequence. The interworkings of the five, properly understood, accounted for all phenomena and all historical events. If the five were not in balance, bad things happened, such as war, plague, and famine.

The Han were expected to conform to basic patterns in everything they did, from conducting their daily lives to performing religious ceremonies to building their cities, palaces, houses, or gardens. They tried to model their structures and their cities after the great cosmic patterns and to respect the *chi*, or divine energy, that flowed through the earth and every object. A builder, for example, did not begin construction without getting advice on selecting a site from a geomancer, a person who performed divination by means of figures, lines, or geographic features. The geomancer took careful measurements of sunlight and shade, the direction of running water, and the lay of the land in general. Whether the site was for a city, a palace, or a garden, the builder would not begin until the geomancer said everything was lined up as it should be. The ideal configuration for a new city was a rectangle, its walls aligned with the four cardinal directions and the administrative district laid out on a north-south axis. This attuned the city and its inhabitants to the basic pattern

of life and helped promote a positive and productive lifestyle within the city walls.

Yang and Yin

At the very heart of Han belief was the concept of yang and yin. To the Chinese, these are the two complementary, primal forces in life. Yang means "sunlit" and is the positive force, masculine in nature, active, warm, dry, bright, and aggressive. Yin means "shaded" and is the negative force, feminine in nature, dark, cool, wet, mysterious, secret, and submissive. To believers, yang and yin are within every natural object. The interplay of the two affects everything in the universe.

To the Han, the sun, Heaven, fire, and good spirits were yang, as were the south side of a hill and the north bank of a river. Horses were yang because they rose front-end first. Men were predominantly yang; they were celestial and of great worth. Shadows, Earth, and evil spirits were yin, as were the north side of a hill and the south bank of a river. Camels were yin because they rose hind-end first. Women were predominantly yin; they were earthly and of no great worth.

The yin power reached its climax in the world at the winter solstice, at which time the emperor would make a sacrifice to Heaven in the south suburb of the capital. The Han considered this the greatest sacrifice of all. It brought back the warm celestial force of yang to draw the new crops out of the wet soil. In midsummer, the yang force peaked and then began to decline and give way to the power of yin.

The correct balance between yang and yin had to be maintained to achieve the perfect life. If the harmony of the two forces were upset, the natural order of things would change for the worse. A person had to think

GREENING YANG

The following hymn is one of eleven Han dynasty poems translated by Anne Birrell and reproduced in *Classical Chinese Literature,* edited by John Minford and Joseph S.M. Lau. The hymn "Greening Yang" is one of a set of seasonal hymns that ritually express the Han cosmological theory of the Five Elements and yin and yang. It describes poetically how yang begins to dominate yin and the cold and gloom of winter are replaced by the life-giving rains and warmth of spring.

> Greening Yang starts to stir,
> Causing root and bulb to obey,
> Its rich moisture loving all alike.
> Padpaw creatures their own ways come forth,
> The sound of thunder brings out flowers' glory.
> Lair-dwellers lean to hear.
> The barren again give birth,
> And so fulfill their destiny.
> All the people rejoice, rejoice.
> Blessings are on the young and pregnant.
> All living things are quickened, quickened.
> Such is the good gift of Spring.

carefully about his actions. Too much yang could cause drought and fire. Too much yin could bring heavy rains and flooding. Life for the Chinese, then, was a constant striving to achieve harmony with nature and not upset the balance of yang and yin.

The Orderliness of Confucianism

The belief in yang and yin and the cosmic forces was in line with Confucianism, which had been the dynasty's official philosophy since about 162 B.C., the twentieth year of the reign of Wudi. The workings and conduct of the government and society, as well as the actions of each person, were based on Confucianism, which emphasized discipline, public service, ceremony, and morality.

At the core of Confucianism was the doctrine of *li,* which indicated the proper conduct in all matters and the right way to behave, believe, and rule. *Li* encouraged standardization and uniformity. Because everyone was supposed to do things the same way, *li* helped Confucianism become ingrained in Chinese politics, society, and culture. According to *The Great Learning,* a work attributed to Confucius, order begins and ends with the cultivation of the individual:

The ancients who wished to illustrate illustrious virtue throughout the kingdom, first ordered well their own states. Wishing to order well their states, they first regulated their families. Wishing to regulate their families, they first cultivated their persons. Wishing to cultivate their persons, they first rectified their hearts. Wishing to rectify their hearts, they first sought to be sincere in their thoughts. Wishing to be sincere in their thoughts, they first extended to the utmost their knowledge. Such extension of knowledge lay in the investigation of things.

Things being investigated, knowledge became complete. Their knowledge being complete, their thoughts were sincere. Their thoughts being sincere, their hearts were then rectified. Their hearts being rectified, their persons were cultivated. Their persons being cultivated, their families were regulated. Their families being regulated, their states were rightly governed. Their states being rightly governed, the whole kingdom was made tranquil and happy.

From the Son of Heaven down to the mass of the people, all must consider the cultivation of the person the root of everything besides.

It cannot be, when the root is neglected, that what should spring from it will be well ordered. It never has been the case that what was of great importance has been slightly cared for, and, at the same time, that what

was of slight importance has been greatly cared for.[17]

In conjunction with the orderliness of li, the practice of doing the right thing, Confucians believed in the idea of jen, which centers on a respect for oneself and for others—a love for humanity. Confucius taught that jen and li should determine all human relationships. In his view, there were five important relationships—ruler and ruled, father and son, husband and wife, older brother and younger brother, and friend and friend. Only friends enjoyed a position of social equality. In the other four relationships, one person was in an inferior position while the other was in a superior position. Those in the inferior position owed respect and obedience to those above them; those in the superior position had to care for and set a good example for those below them.

Confucians believed that carrying out the proper conduct in each of the five relationships fulfilled the requirements of jen and li. This, they believed, would result in a just society that functioned smoothly because people knew their place in society and acted for its welfare rather than for their own selfish interests. French historian and sinologist (a person versed in Chinese history, art, and literature) René Grousset explains that these are the basic beliefs on which all of Confucianism was centered:

> Confucius . . . refused to probe into the mysteries of destiny. . . . "Recognize," he said, "that you know what you know, and that you are ignorant of what you do not know." And again, "If you do not know about the living, how can you know about the dead?" His teaching recognizes no difference

THE WILL OF HEAVEN

Tung Chung-shu was a reknowned Confucian and the chief scholar of the imperial university during the period of the Western Han. In this translation by Burton Watson of a portion of "Deep Significance of the Spring and Autumn Annals," from William Theodore de Bary and Irene Bloom's *Sources of Chinese Tradition,* Tung Chung-shu explains the difference between portents and wonders, both of which are signs from Heaven. According to Tung Chung-shu, understanding these will help a person interpret the will of Heaven.

The creatures of Heaven and earth at times display unusual changes and these are called wonders. Lesser ones are called ominous portents. The portents always come first and are followed by wonders. Portents are Heaven's warnings, wonders are Heaven's threats. Heaven first sends warnings, and if men do not understand, then it sends wonders to awe them. This is what the Book of Odes means when it says: "We tremble at the awe and the fearfulness of Heaven!" The genesis of all such portents and wonders is a direct result of errors in the state. When the first indications of error begin to appear in the state, Heaven sends forth ominous portents and calamities to warn men and announce the fact. If, in spite of these warnings and announcements, men still do not realize how they have gone wrong, then Heaven sends prodigies and wonders to terrify them. If, after these terrors, men still know no awe or fear, then calamity and misfortune will visit them. From this we may see that the will of Heaven is benevolent, for it has no desire to trap or betray mankind.

If we examine these wonders and portents carefully, we may discern the will of Heaven. The will of Heaven desires us to do certain things and not to do others. As to those things which Heaven wishes and does not wish, if a man searches within himself, he will surely find warnings of them in his own heart, and if he looks about him at daily affairs, he will find verification of these warnings in the state. Thus we can discern the will of Heaven in these portents and wonders. We should not hate such signs, but stand in awe of them, considering that Heaven wishes to repair our faults and save us from our errors. Therefore it takes this way to warn us.

between individual morality and civic and social morality. Its aim lies in the good government of the people, assured . . . by a harmony of the virtue of the prince and the order of Heaven. "It is the moral power of the sovereign, the supernatural influence which he draws from the mandate of Heaven, which makes for the good or evil conduct of his people." . . .

If we had to condense the spirit of Confucianism into a single formula, we would say that it is a civic order in communion, or rather in collaboration, with the cosmic order.[18]

The Individualism of Daoism

Even though Confucianism was the official ideology, the Han also permitted other religions and philosophies to influence their thinking, including some popular superstitions and mysticism. One such influence was Daoism, the school of the "Way," the only religion of China born and developed in China. Originating from sorcery and supernatural divination, Daoism took shape in the late Western Han period.

Both a philosophy and a religion, Daoism looked inward, seeking harmony with nature. It emphasized individualism and naturalness, discouraged conventional social customs, and favored tolerance. Daoists believed that civilization was corrupt and that humanity needed simplicity and closeness to nature. According to the philosophy, Dao, the "Way," created the universe, maintains it, and represents the fluctuating reality that is existence. The Daoist wise man, or sage, sought to come into full harmony with the "Way." He did this by rejecting human con-

ventions not in accord with the natural order. Daoists also believed that a life lived according to the Dao was a healthy human life. Some Daoists sought immortality through magic, breath control, and alchemy.

Most experts credit a Zhou sage named Laozi, the "Master," with writing the greatest work of Daoism, *Dao de jing* (*Classic of the Way of Power*). A small book of about five thousand words, the *Dao* is the foundation of Daoist religious thought. It discusses many philosophical and practical issues, such as the origin and workings of the universe, the laws that govern the change and movement of things, the correct way to live and behave, and the way to govern a state. Chinese scholars of all ages long after the

Laozi, the founder of Daoism, rides an ox as his servant follows on foot.

ON THE NATURE OF DAO

Liu An, who died in 122 B.C., was the prince of Huainan and the grandson of Gaozu, the founder of the Han dynasty. Liu An was also a student of Daoism who spent much of his time engaging in alchemy and looking for an elixir that would make humans immortal. This translation by Herbert Giles, which appears in John Minford and Joseph S.M. Lau's anthology *Classical Chinese Literature*, is from a book bearing Liu An's name compiled by scholars at his court. It describes the power and changing nature of Dao and explains the role Dao played in bringing about civilization.

Dao roofs over the sky and is the foundation of the earth; it extends north, south, east, and west, stretching to the eight extreme points in those directions. Its height is beyond reach and its depth is unfathomable; it enfolds both the sky and the earth, and produces things which had been formless. It is like the flow of a spring, which starts bubbling up from nothing but gradually forms a volume of rushing muddy water which again gradually becomes clear. Therefore, if set vertically, it will block all the space between the sky and the earth; if set laterally, it will touch the shores of the Four Seas; inexhaustible by use, it knows neither the fullness of morning nor the decay of night; dispersed, it fills space; compressed, it is scarce a handful; scant, it can be ample; dark, it can be light; weak, it can be strong; soft, it can be hard. Though open on all sides, it contains the two cosmological Principles; it binds up the universe, while making manifest the sun, moon, and stars; it is thick as clay, and yet is watery; it is infinitesimally fine, and yet it can be subdivided; it makes mountains rise high and valleys sink low; it makes beasts to walk, birds to fly, the sun and moon to shine, the stars to move, the unicorn to come forth, and the phoenix to hover above us.

The First Two Emperors of old obtained control of Dao, and established themselves in the center of all things, and by their divine influence brought about civilization and gave peace to the world. Thus, the sky duly turned round, while the earth stood still, and the wheel of human life revolved without ceasing.

time of Laozi studied and interpreted the book. But there is no concrete evidence proving that Laozi wrote it or even that he actually existed.

In 1973, archaeologists working in Mawangdui in the eastern suburbs of Changsha in China's Hunan province discovered two copies of the *Dao de jing* written on silk. These were much earlier versions than the ones scholars already possessed. In 1996, archaeologists found a manuscript of the "Dao" in a tomb in Jingmen City in Hubei province that is different from other known manuscripts of the work. Whereas the others were written in a style similar to a poem, this one is in dialogue form, much like the writings of Confucius. Because Confucian dialogues were used as political as well as social instruction, some modern scholars believe that early Daoism was not just a form of nature worship but also a philosophy on how to govern the state. Some experts have interpreted the dialogue form of the manuscript as evidence that it was used in a classroom, probably to teach governing principles to young bureaucrats.

Buddhism

The third religion or philosophy to influence Han thinking was Buddhism. Historians agree that Buddhism flowered in China during the time of the Eastern Han. They do not agree, however, on when it first entered China or how it arrived. Some historians believe that Buddhism came to China during the rule of the Western Han; others claim it did not appear until the second period of Han rule. At the same time, some historians claim Buddhism came directly from India, while others argue that it came mainly from the oasis kingdoms of Central Asia and found its way to China slowly along the Silk Road.

Academician and translator Raymond Dawson relates the most popular story about how Buddhism first came to China:

> According to a famous story, the apocryphal character of which has only been recognized in modern times, the Han emperor Ming (reigned A.D. 58–75) once dreamed that he saw a "golden man". When he was informed that must be the foreign god named Buddha, he sent an embassy to India in order to obtain the sacred texts. After several years the envoys returned together with two Indian masters, for whom the emperor founded the *Pai-ma-ssu* or "White Horse Monastery" at the capital Loyang. Thus the Good Law was introduced into China. Although this is no more than a pious legend, it may contain a memory of the existence of Buddhism at the time of the emperor Ming, for the first actual mention of Buddhism in reliable historical sources is connected with the activities of an imperial prince in northern Kiangsu, in the year A.D. 65.[19]

The White Horse Monastery in the story is still in existence today in the Chinese city of Luoyang in the province of Henan. It is the earliest monastery established in China and has a long history. It was named after the legendary white horse that carried Buddhist scripture to the monastery.

Buddhism was based on the teachings of Siddhartha Gautama, a prince born in 563 B.C. in what is now Nepal. Many stories and legends have circulated about his life

A statue of the Buddha from the Yungang caves of China.

and about how he came to be the Buddha, the "Enlightened One." According to the most popular legend, Siddhartha left his home and his family to find religious peace and the way to salvation. Finally, at the age of thirty-five, after many years of searching and religious meditation, he discovered why people were suffering and found a way of escaping it. The truth he had been seeking could be summed up in the two ideas of self-culture and universal love. From that point in time, he became known as the Buddha.

Buddhism taught that life is suffering, caused by the desire for things to be different from the way they are. Suffering, however, does not have to be endless. Following the Middle Way of moderation and the Eightfold Path (Right Views, Right Intentions, Right Speech, Right Action, Right Occupation, Right Effort, Right Concentration, and Right Meditation) will bring suffering to an end.

Although Buddhism appealed to all social classes during the Han dynasty, the upper classes especially found it attractive because it was intellectually sophisticated and artistically pleasing. Buddhism explained the loss of their society and comforted them.

The Han Synthesis

The Han realized that trying to adhere strictly to one philosophy to the exclusion of all others was a mistake. The Qin had tried that, and it had weakened rather than strengthened the dynasty. Instead, Han thinkers chose to try to unify rival schools of Chinese thought and philosophy by incorporating certain beliefs and practices of each. According to scholar Edward Craig, "The intellectual orthodoxy which came to dominance in the Han dynasty was a river fed by three powerful streams: Confucianism, Daoism, and Buddhism."[20]

THE MYTHICAL DRAGON

The ancient Chinese valued a number of mythical creatures. One was the firebird, the phoenix, consumed by its own flames and reborn from its ashes as part of a regular cycle. Another mythical creature was the dragon, the divine lord of the waters, which the Qin emperor Shi huangdi made his emblem. In his work *Deities and Demons of the Far East*, sculptor, artist, and poet Brian P. Katz describes how the dragon was perceived by the ancient Chinese.

> According to legend, the dragon had the head of a camel; the horns of a deer; the eyes of a demon; the ears of a cow; the long whiskers of a cat; the long neck of a snake; the belly of a frog; the scales of a carp; the talons of an eagle; and the paws of a tiger. Dragons were believed to have been deaf. Most dragons were not winged, but had fins for swimming that were (understandably) mistaken for wings.
>
> The scales on the dragon's body signified universal harmony. In all, the dragon had 117 scales. Eighty-one scales were under the yang influence, good fortune; and thirty-six scales were under the yin influence, bad fortune. The dragon was a creature of both active and reactive powers, part preserver and part eliminator.
>
> Dragons inhabited bodies of water—the larger the body of water, the more powerful the dragon. They controlled the dispensing of rains, and created thunder by rolling large pearls in the heavens. They were seen as both water gods and the guardians of pearls. Dragons were also the bearers of wealth and good fortune. Each town believed in its own local dragon.
>
> The Chinese believed that there were heavenly dragons as well as earthly dragons. Those in heaven resided in the part of the sky known as the palace of the Green Dragon. (It was given this title by the Chinese astronomers who studied the constellation of the dragon.)
>
> Some dragons pulled the chariots of many emperors, as well as the chariot of the sun. There were also many dragon kings, known as lung wang, throughout China's mythological history.

A porcelain jar with the dragon motif.

Confucianism remained the dominant philosophy under the Han, but it was a Confucianism integrated with and tempered by Daoist, Buddhist, and other philosophical thought. For example, the Han system of thought took in the yin-yang cosmology of the naturalists; the Daoist desire to recognize and be in harmony with the order of nature; Confucian teachings on caring government, rule by virtuous leaders, and respect for learning; and Legalist principles of administration and economic development. The belief that the emperor was to live as an example of compassion and kindness and to care for the welfare of his people came from the teachings of Confucius, while the belief that the emperor should act withdrawn from active rule came from Daoist teachings.

The Han succeeded in their attempt to blend all the alternate schools of thought into a single system, much as they succeeded in the larger project of unifying Chinese government. In fact, many modern scholars consider this unification into a single coherent, orderly, and structured system the most enduring Han legacy of all. They doubt that the Han would have been able to accomplish the degree of unity they did without fusing into one virtually all of the major philosophies of the times.

CHAPTER FOUR

A SINGLE AND SUPREME RULER

The rebel who ascended the throne of the Chinese empire in 202 B.C. as the first Han emperor was known as Liu Bang. Liu was his family name and Bang his personal name—the names he had received at birth. Once he became emperor, however, use of his personal name was forbidden, and he became known as *huangdi*, the Dread Lord. When he died, he became known by another name, Gaozu—his posthumous, or temple, name used in Confucian rites. The same sense of order in the naming of the Han ruler was reflected in the Han social structure. It was laid out in the shape of a pyramid. At the apex—the very top—of this pyramid was the emperor, a man unlike any other mortal, so sacred that he stood above and apart from all others.

A Regimented Existence

The emperor led a life very different from that of anyone else in the empire, a life ordained by ritual and regimented by an inflexible code of behavior. Everything to do with the emperor was steeped in protocol, and the penalty for not observing that protocol could be death. No one was allowed to make eye contact with the emperor. Those in his presence knew not to rest their gaze higher than the foot of the stairs below

his throne. His subjects dared not speak or write his name. Even his ministers were not allowed to address him directly. Any messages the ministers might have were passed to imperial attendants posted at the base of the royal dais—or raised platform—that held the throne. The attendants, in turn, passed on the messages to the emperor.

Rules prevailed even in the selection of the emperor's wife and concubines. During the eighth month of each year, palace officials selected the new women for the emperor's harem. Only the most beautiful, elegant, and respectable teenage virgins were picked to be imperial concubines. Those chosen were divided into fourteen ranks, which later were reduced to three—honorable lady, beautiful lady, and chosen lady. The empress herself generally came from among the concubines of the imperial harem. The number of concubines and wives varied with each emperor. Emperor Wudi, for example, was said to have had as many as one thousand concubines in his harem.

For the Han, the harem was a status symbol, just one of many enjoyed by the emperor. There were also unique clothing and jewelry that only he was allowed to wear and heavily gilded carriages in which only he could ride. Guards cleared the roads on

Comfortable in his palanquin, the emperor is borne on the shoulders of his faithful retinue.

which the emperor was traveling of any other traffic, and no one but the emperor could use the middle entrance of each gateway to the capital city.

The emperor held the power of life and death in his hands. Anyone ignoring palace protocol paid a heavy price. Being caught trespassing onto palace grounds meant immediate death. A noble who in a moment of anger cursed the emperor was chopped in two. The emperor did not have to explain why he chose to have someone killed. When he gave an order, it was carried out without hesitation or question.

Rule and Responsibility

With privilege and power, however, came expectations. The emperor had to fulfill these expectations and carry out certain duties. In verse XII:19 of the *Analects*, Confucius wrote, "The way the wind blows, that is the way the grass bends." For the Han, this meant that the emperor was responsible for the well-being of his people and for setting an example of moral virtue. Historian Michael Loewe explains the emperor's duty:

The emperor [was] the unique source of temporal authority and leadership. He owed his position partly to his own merits and character, and, in theory, to the trust and responsibility implanted in him by a non-earthy authority, who was designated in Chinese thought and writing as "Heaven." The emperor was regarded as being

A TASTE OF THE RICH LIFE

Emperor Wudi was known for his love of luxury and lavish living. In his work *Chinese Civilization*, Marcel Granet uses descriptions based on the writings of such Han historians as Sima Qian in his discussion of the Han dynasty. This description paints a vivid picture of the entertainments provided at feasts Wudi gave in his palaces at Chang'an.

His eunuchs command companies of jugglers and musicians. His harem contains a crowd of singers and dancers; the cleverest become empresses or favorites. . . . A vast building, the palace Kia-yi is completely furnished for opera. There the great jousts take place, whence arise the Chinese theater. Mechanicians are able to show snow falling and clouds rising there, while the tumult of storms, the rolling of thunder, and flashes of lightning make the majestic power of Heaven appear quite close. Processions of the Immortals or of strange Beasts pass, alternating with mountebanks, who climb poles or lift weights. Jugglers swallow swords, spit fire, make water spurt from the earth by tracing drawings on it, play with serpents, while women with long sleeves, clothed in gauze and painted, dance the most lascivious of their dances, and whilst at the top of a mast, perched on a carriage, acrobats hang by their feet, or wheel around it indefinitely, shooting arrows in all directions . . . everywhere where the Majesty of the Emperor should triumph. Hunts and fishing excursions are also the occasion of triumphal galas.

Figurines of a group of four entertainers, whose job it would have been to divert the Han emperor on command.

the son of Heaven, and he was thought of as the intermediary of Heaven in its relationship with earth. The mandate bestowed by Heaven on its son conferred the right to expect obedience and loyalty from the inhabitants of the earth, and the power to preside over the authority that was needed for earth's government. But with this privilege the mandate coupled responsibility for the physical well-being and prosperity of the earth's inhabitants, and a readiness on the part of the incumbent to deport himself in a way that was worthy of the unique position that he occupied.[21]

The Han scholar Tung Chung-shu, who believed in rigid mathematical proportion in social arrangements, clearly defined the emperor's responsibilities, dividing them into three parts. These parts corresponded to Tung Chung-shu's belief that Heaven, Earth, and man formed a triad. The emperor, he said, ruled by the decree of Heaven and was responsible for maintaining Heaven, Earth, and man in harmony. According to Tung Chung-shu,

> He [the emperor] makes the sacrifice (to Heaven) in the suburb [of the capital city] with utmost respect;
> He serves his forefathers in the ancestral shrines;
> He elevates and illuminates both filial and fraternal piety;
> He displays what is unique in filial conduct.
> By these means he honors the Heavenly base.
> He holds the ritual plow and tills in person;

> He gathers the mulberry and tends the silk worms himself;
> He breaks ground and clears it away— for adequate clothing and food.
> By these means he honors the Earthly base.
> He founds a Round Academy and village centers of learning;
> He cultivates filial and fraternal piety, respect and deference;
> He enlightens through instruction and conversion;
> He inspires by ceremony and music.
> By these means he honors the Human base.[22]

Tung Chung-shu's concept of the triad and the emperor's role of maintaining harmony remained the prevailing belief long after the rule of the Han was over.

The Royal Palace

Clearly, in the eyes of the Han, the emperor was unique, far different from all other members of society. The living quarters of the emperor, therefore, had to be different from those of all other members of society as well. They had to be created especially for the emperor, separate from the rest of the community and designed to enhance the nobility and power of the royal house. As a result, the emperor was housed in a complex of extremely luxurious palaces.

An emperor had more than one palace, each with at least one audience hall. The only way to gain entrance to the palace was through special gateways. To further ensure privacy and protection, the palace was bordered by watchtowers in which sentinels stood guard. No one thought much about what the palaces cost to build or maintain.

A jade model of a palace gate guarded by sentinels and crowned with watchtowers.

The main concern was the luxury of the buildings and the surrounding areas and the comfort of the emperor and nobles who occupied them. Only the most perfect materials were used, and only the most skilled builders, craftsmen, and artisans were hired to design the palaces. Thousands of laborers were put to work constructing them.

In these elegant palaces, the emperor lived apart from the rest of the world. According to historian Michael Loewe, the emperor "dwelt in the innermost part of a palace, which was discreetly veiled from the prying eyes of an onlooker, protected from criminals and bandits, and secluded from the baneful influences of lowly or untoward inhabitants of the earth."[23] Although this separation from the everyday, commonplace world served to emphasize the imperial status, it led to a lonely,

isolated life for the emperor. His was a highly sheltered existence even though he was surrounded by people. Other than during solemn councils, receptions, and ceremonies, his main contact was with people in his court. Thus, his relationships were confined to his closest and most faithful advisers and officials; slaves and other servants; trusted eunuchs, castrated men who generally served as palace chamberlains and worked within the women's apartments; courtiers who waited in daily attendance; and females of the court, consorts, concubines, and mothers. Also living within the palace walls were people employed to oversee religious duties, prepare the emperor's food and medicines, and make sure that younger members of the family were brought up properly.

Han writers wrote often of the splendor of the emperors' palace complexes that took up so much of the capital, or royal city. During the Western Han, the royal city was Chang'an, located on the Wei River in the present-day Shanxi province near the city of Xian. The first Han emperor, Gaozu, chose the site for Chang'an, which over time served as the capital city for eleven different dynasties. There, Gaozu built two huge palace complexes—Changle and Weiyang. Both sat high in the southern part of the city, along with an arsenal. For the most part, the dowager empresses lived in the Changle complex, the "Palace of Eternal Joy." The Weiyang complex, with its forty-some buildings, covered at least one-fifth of the city. Within the complex were private apartments for the emperor and the empress and the ladies of the court, along with libraries and the temple of the ancestors. Raised, roof-covered passageways linked the different buildings of the complex. Steps and a ramp for the emperor's carriage

THE ROYAL CITY

The Western Han capital city of Chang'an is said to have rivaled Rome both in splendor and in size. During the height of Western Han rule, it was home to hundreds of thousands of people. Archaeological digs in Chang'an and in the Eastern Han capital of Luoyang, along with the replicas of buildings found in tombs, help contemporary scholars form a clearer picture of ancient cities. Excavations at Chang'an, for example, have shown that wooden bridges crossed a moat that ran around the city's perimeter. The bridges led to twelve gates spaced at intervals in the thick walls of rammed earth. According to histories of the time, men and women labored for four years on the almost fifty-three-foot-wide stamped earth and brick walls that reached about forty feet high. When the laborers finished, the total distance around the wall was nearly forty-eight miles.

The first Han emperor, Gaozu, chose the site for Chang'an with great care, making sure the cosmic principles were right. The Han believed that a capital city properly designed in accordance with cosmic principles would magically compel all the emperor's subject peoples to adopt the Chinese civilization. According to Han writers, the emperor had Chang'an built to face south so that when he sat in his audience chamber he would face the direction of the domain of the yang that marked the sun's highest position in the heavens. In his "Ode to the West Capital," first-century Han astronomer, philosopher, and historian Zhang Heng proclaimed with admiration, "For his [the emperor's] purpose, he took thought of the spirits of Heaven and Earth that he might suitably determine the place that was to be the Heavenly City." The Han historian Ban Gu also told of his satisfaction with the celestial layout of the city and its great palaces: "Their frame and image were matched with Heaven and Earth. Their warp-lines and weft-lines were matched with yin and yang."

Riches, extravagance, and luxury were the hallmarks of Chang'an, whose palaces took up about two-thirds of the city's land. Services were held at its principal shrines. Here, too, the emperor received the annual homage and tribute from marquises, the highest rank of the realm, and performed the ceremony that gave kings authority to rule their domains. South of the city, the emperor worshiped Heaven at a circular altar, placed in the quarter where the yang was dominant.

led up a terrace to a massive audience chamber more than eleven hundred feet long and almost five hundred feet wide.

In all, there were five royal complexes in Chang'an, each with palaces several stories high and towered gateways. They were built mostly of timber and had plastered walls painted white or scarlet. Many of the inside walls were faced with wood or covered with paintings or silk hangings. It is believed that the beams, capitals, and jade-based columns of the palaces were made of scented or painted woods and adorned with ornaments made of metal or semiprecious stones. According to Han historians, luxurious and elegant imperial gardens with ornamental towers, man-made lakes, and exotic animals adjoined the palaces.

Much of original Chang'an was destroyed in fighting and fires from A.D. 9 to 27 and from 190 to 195. Today, not much of the city itself remains—only a few sections of wall and some rammed earth terraces. However, amid the debris, archaeologists did find scattered semicircular roof tiles. They believe that because the tiles had been sealed with circular end pieces for decorative purposes, they must have projected out over the eaves. Even with their limited findings, archaeologists have been able to get a fairly accurate idea of the city and some of its palaces. Archaeologists who have been excavating at Chang'an off and on since 1959 have also been able to reconstruct some of the palaces and other buildings. Their work has helped modern-day scholars and experts better understand the architecture of the palaces at Chang'an.

The Emperor's Mausoleum

Palaces, privileges, and power were not the only outward signs of the distinctive nature

The ruins of a Han Dynasty wall in Tun-huang, China. Similar ruins have been excavated at Chang'an.

of the emperor's person. Equally revealing is the majestic mausoleum in which the emperor's mortal remains were laid to rest. Because the emperor was considered divine, the liaison between Heaven and the people, his burial had to be much more spectacular than that of ordinary mortals.

The Han believed in an afterlife that was a continuation of a person's life on earth. For the Han, an emperor's burial chamber was his afterworld headquarters and, as such, had to equal the splendor of his residence on earth. Tomb excavations during the last fifty years have provided evidence of this belief, clearly showing the position an emperor held in Han society and the magnificent trappings with which he was surrounded during his reign.

Yangling, the mausoleum of the fourth Western Han emperor Jingdi and his wife Empress Wang, bears this out. The mausoleum is part of a symmetrically constructed tomb complex located about fifteen miles

AN UNUSUAL PALACE

In 2001, Chinese archaeologists made an exciting discovery at the site of the Western Han capital city of Chang'an. According to Xinhua News Agency, the official news source of the government of the People's Republic of China, archaeologists discovered that Gui Palace, which housed Han empresses and concubines, had underground chambers. According to the March 7, 2001, article "Chinese Empresses, Imperial Concubines Live in Unusual Palace 2,000 Years Ago," the Han was the only dynasty in Chinese history to build a special palace for empresses and imperial concubines.

The Gui Palace, used for more than 100 years from the middle to the end of the Western Han Dynasty (206 B.C.–A.D. 24), was jointly unearthed by Chinese and Japanese archaeologists over the past four years.

"Underground buildings have rarely been found in Chinese palaces in history," said Liu Qingzhu, director of the Institute of Archaeology under the Chinese Academy of Social Sciences.

"It's too early to make a conclusion about the use of the newly found buildings. We only know they were not used for recreational or living purposes. Maybe the rooms were used only for important imperial activities," Liu said.

According to Li Yufang, head of the archaeological team, the Gui Palace has a haphazard design, but the whole palace is now under strict protection.

Liu Qingzhu said that Han was the only dynasty in Chinese history to build a special palace for empresses and imperial concubines, while the living places for queens of other dynasties were included in the imperial palaces.

"Women in the palace also participated in politics. Research of the queens' palace will help us understand more about the role of women in politics in Chinese history," said Liu.

north of the present-day city of Xian on Wuling Yuan Plain, the burial place of nine Han emperors. In addition to the mausoleum, which covers what would have been about one-third of Chang'an, the complex includes the tomb of the empress, the tomb of Jingdi's favorite concubine, ritual constructions, and more than eighty satellite tombs. The different-sized satellite tombs, which reach out in all directions, have yielded more than sixty thousand burial objects, including porcelain documents, copper coins, lacquerwares, and relics made of porcelain, bronze, and jade.

In March 1990, workers building a highway near Jingdi's tomb noticed irregularities in the soil. They called the archaeologists at the Shaanxi Institute of Archaeology, who unearthed twenty-four pits near Jingdi's tomb. Each pit seemed to have a different theme, so the archaeologists thought that from them they could learn about different aspects of Han life. In 1991, archaeologist Wang Xueli and his team found pieces of terra-cotta figures at the site. According to an article that appeared that year in *Time International* magazine, soil samples showed that robbers had broken into the tomb about two thousand years earlier and had abandoned it after removing all the gold and silver. The article also described Wang's team's discoveries:

> By the time of the Han dynasty, the practice of entombing both humans and animals alive with the deceased Emperor had long since ceased. But the rite was continued symbolically. Like a magnificent dollhouse, the vaults were peopled with tens of thousands of miniature terracotta figures symbolizing every aspect of the Emperor's life. Wang's team has recovered fragments of 600 warriors . . . as well as fragments of wooden chariots and horses. There are also farmers, servants and children; charmingly modeled cows, pigs, lambs and chickens; farming and household utensils; even miniature pots and pans. No de-

tail was spared; soldiers were equipped with a tiny sword at their waist, a spear in their left hand and a shield in their right.[24]

When archaeologists began unearthing rows of terra-cotta figures that had been placed in underground chambers, they excavated ninety naked and armless male and female figures, each about two feet tall, with about fifteen different facial expressions, from smiling to frowning. They also found bits of silk and hemp cloth in the soil, indicating that the figures originally had been clothed. The find was impressive in many ways, as B.K. Davis explains in the article "The Chinese Emperors' Eternal Armies":

> Jingdi's warriors show the beauty of the nude figure beneath. Once fired, they were fitted with wooden arms that rotated at the shoulder, then painted and fitted with silk uniforms, red headbands, and red lacquered leggings. Over the centuries the figures were damaged as wooden ceilings and pillars collapsed. Wooden arms and silk uniforms have rotted away over the centuries. . . .
>
> Above and beyond any other legacies . . . emperors may have left behind, their terracotta armies survive as incredible works of art. Intricate details in armor, facial features, rank insignia, and positioning offer us a rich library of historic information and a peek into a segment of life in the early years of the Chinese empire.[25]

Since then, archaeologists have found many more pits guarding the tombs of Jingdi and his empress. They have unearthed more

The ruins of Jiaohe in Xingjiang, China. Han cities often reflected the authority and isolation of the emperor.

than six hundred terra-cotta cavalry and foot soldiers, as well as livestock, work tools, and many wooden chariots. Among these were hundreds of female warriors armed and mounted on horseback, which some archaeologists believe are the oldest female terracotta figures found in any tombs in China. Archaeologists remain divided about the role of the women. Some believe the women were part of a ceremonial procession. Others argue that the obviously female figures are armed and in a military formation and were made expressly to show that Han women took part in battles.

Archaeological excavations have proven that more than ten thousand prisoners built the mausoleum, which in reality was more of an underground palace. A farmer digging a reservoir led archaeologists to excavate further when he found bones scattered on a piece of land near the mausoleum. The excavation revealed that the place had been a graveyard for thousands of mausoleum builders, whose heads and bodies were buried in different places. According to

the head of the archaeological team that unearthed the prisoners, during the twenty-eight years it took to build Jingdi's mausoleum many prisoners were killed for resisting or for trying to escape.

In February 2001 Chinese archaeologists made yet another find at Jingdi's mausoleum. They discovered chessboard-shaped residential quarters and eleven interconnecting roads running east-west and north-south. Archaeologists believe the discovery will be of great value to their study of ancient Chinese cities.

Archaeologists already have shown that certain Han cities, such as Chang'an, were royal cities built to the whim and desire of the emperor, carefully planned and laid out to please the gods. They were a reflection of the isolation and superiority of the emperor and evidence of his supremacy during his lifetime—just as his mausoleum was a reflection of the high esteem in which he had been held and the quality of life he had led, both of which were expected to be carried into the afterlife.

CHAPTER FIVE

A BUREAUCRACY BASED ON MERIT

On the wall of a tomb unearthed in the modern Chinese province of Hopei, archaeologists discovered the image of a man painted in black, scarlet, and blue on a yellow background. The man wore robes and a sword and was carrying a writing tablet. He was a Han dynasty official who lived around A.D. 182 during the time of the Eastern Han. The basic system of a strong central government created by the Han rested on bureaucrats and officials like this man.

Under the Han dynasty, the civil service contained close to 150,000 officials with many different ranks and degrees of status. This was in keeping with the Han theory of bureaucracy, which was still in practice well into the twentieth century. Officials like the one in the tomb painting were a mainstay of the Han dynasty. As an official, the man was a member of the group of individuals who served as the empire's scholars, civil servants, and statesmen—the complex and efficient bureaucracy that drove the Han's system of strong central government.

The Civil Service

In Han China, bureaucrats and officials were the acknowledged leaders of society. They set the pace of cultural achievement for the entire empire. They were the reason the Chinese developed the education system they did. Education probably was more advanced in Han China than anywhere else in the known world at that time. But it had a special purpose: to train future members of the civil service, to turn promising boys and young men into "learned and upright government officials."

To the Han, education and centralized government went hand in hand. Although they had adopted the Qin tradition of centralization of power, the Han soon recognized that an emperor did not—could not—run so vast an empire without skilled, knowledgeable help. It would take many bureaucrats and officials to keep the widespread empire running smoothly. The result was an extremely complex structure of offices.

Chinese writers and statesmen of the time described the institutions of their empire. In their writings, they tell what happened over time as the Han tried to establish a civil service that could organize many of the activities of their government. Until the Han came into power, bureaucrats and officials did not have to prove they were knowledgeable or capable to be appointed to an office. Most got their positions for reasons other than suitability or merit. The emperor may have taken a personal liking to them, for example, or someone influential or close to the emperor may have recommended them. A candidate had to have the right connections. If his grandfather, father, uncle, or other close relative was a high official, he was almost certain to get the official post he wanted.

It was also not uncommon for someone to buy an official post. This happened even in the very early years of the Han dynasty. However, this meant that a Chinese who wanted a career in government had to be very wealthy. Even the most unimportant posts could cost as much as 100,000 cash. (Cash was the name given to the round bronze coins with a hole in the center that had been introduced by Qin Shi huangdi and that were to remain in use for more than two thousand years.) It was not surprising, then, that many officials and bureaucrats did not have the skills or the motivation they needed to do their jobs.

A Structured Bureaucracy Based on Confucian Scholarship

The Han changed the system by setting certain criteria to select bureaucrats and officials. They established a civil service based on Confucian ideals. And that changed the way the Chinese empire was run. Many historians agree with the opinion stated by academician Kenneth Scott Latourette in his work *The Chinese: Their History and Culture:* "The device of a bureaucracy recruited through civil service examinations was one of the most noteworthy inventions of the Chinese."[26] According to Confucius, government service should be based on ability, not on imperial impulse, wealth, or the social position into which one was born. In

A Confucian manuscript, created during the early years of the Han Dynasty.

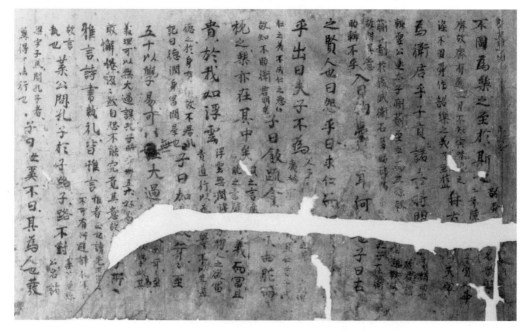

THE FIVE CLASSICS

To become an official or a bureaucrat in Han China, it was necessary to have studied and demonstrated a knowledge of the five classics of Confucianism: *Yijing*, *Shujing*, *Shijing*, *Chunqiu*, and *Liji*. All five of these classics were works from the Zhou dynasty that were collected and edited by members of the original Confucian school.

The *Yijing*, or *The Book of Changes*, contains the concept of the universe moving in cycles. The path of change was traced through sixty-four distinct stages, each represented pictorially by a hexagram in the book. The Zhou used the hexagrams to predict the future. When the sixty-fourth stage was completed, the cycle started all over again. Thus, the universe was always in a state of change. The Chinese thought of people, time, and life in terms of these cycles.

The *Shujing*, or *The Book of Documents*, is considered the earliest work of history and political science in Chinese history. The collection of documents that make up the work show history as a process of change and present it as a way for people to study past events and learn from them. The *Shujing* also introduces the concept of the Mandate of Heaven, the doctrine based on a belief that rulers are chosen by Heaven because they are virtuous and worthy to rule. If a ruler is overthrown, it is either because he did something that was not virtuous and lost the mandate to rule or because someone more virtuous had come to power.

The *Shijing*, or *The Book of Odes*, is a collection of poems and songs of all types from many different sources. It includes everything from political protests to drinking songs to love poems.

The *Chunqiu*, or *Spring and Autumn Annals*, consists of events that took place from 782 B.C. to 481 B.C. in the home state of Confucius.

The *Liji*, or *The Book of Rites*, regulates interpersonal behavior and instructs the reader how to behave under almost every circumstance and in almost every situation conceivable.

A bureaucrat was expected to have mastered the wisdom in all of these texts. His enlightened understanding of the fundamental principles within the classics was to help him rule in accordance with ancient precepts and not by the whim of his own judgment.

his work *Zhong Yong,* or *The Doctrine of the Mean,* Confucius offers these guidelines for government and officials:

> With the right men the growth of government is rapid, just as vegetation is rapid in the earth; and, moreover, their government might be called an easily-growing rush. . . .
>
> Therefore the administration of government lies in getting proper men. Such men are to be got by means of the ruler's own character. That character is to be cultivated by his treading in the ways of duty. And the treading those ways of duty is to be cultivated by the cherishing of benevolence.[27]

Confucius was not the only one who believed this. As early as the fifth century B.C., philosophers advised that the highest offices of state not be given to men just because they had been born into the nobility. Such offices, they argued, should be given to men of ability, men with both moral integrity and intellectual capacity.

In keeping with their state ideology of Confucianism, the Han established a highly structured paid bureaucracy based on scholarship. Under the new system, candidates for a position had to prove their merit by taking civil service examinations that tested their knowledge of Confucian teachings. Those who became officials had to conform to Confucian values of proper behavior and personal integrity when they were serving the emperor and the state. They had to run the government in accord with the ideals of Confucianism. The focus by all students, bureaucrats, and officials on the Confucian ideology created a uniformity of thought and action among civil servants. This uni-

formity assured the government of consistency. Equally important, Confucian ideals filtered down and influenced the rest of Han society. The adherence to a single set of principles helped unify China and make it as much a cultural whole as a political one.

The Han carefully structured the administrative levels of their government in pyramid form, with bureaucrats at each level performing specific administrative tasks. At the lowest level—the base of the pyramid—were hamlets, each made up of a few unrelated families or a number of families from the same clan. At the next level were communes and districts. Directly above these were county-sized prefectures, above which were state-sized commanderies. At the very top of the pyramid was the emperor, with his cabinet just slightly below. Three imperial advisers ranked directly below the emperor. One was the chancellor, who was in charge of finance. Another was the commander in chief of the military. The third was the imperial counselor, who headed the bureaucracy, which in the year A.D. 1 was 130,000 strong. Under these three imperial advisers were nine cabinet-level ministers whose responsibilities ranged from the imperial purse to the royal stables.

With more than enough local men who wanted to be bureaucrats or officials, the government faced the challenge of proper selection. Higher ranks had to decide which of the new petitioners were educated enough and trustworthy enough to handle the grave responsibilities of administration. The government also had to ensure that rich men who were not qualified could not buy their way into the civil service. The Han needed men who had demonstrated that they could not be tempted by bribes or other entice-

A group of civil servants flanked by soldiers kneels before the emperor's palace.

ments. Officials and bureaucrats had to be men who could be trusted not to abuse their positions to serve their own interests.

Despite the rigors of the selection process, the quality of official society varied a great deal over the four hundred years the Han ruled China. Some years the officials were too authoritative. Others they were not authoritative enough. Some officials gave in to temptation and allowed themselves to be corrupted. There were instances when men whose abilities had not yet been tested got appointments because they had been sponsored by a family close to the emperor or by someone influential. But, even at their worst, the officials were preferable to the alternative. Without an official administration, violence and lawlessness were more likely to break out.

Recruiting and Training a Large Bureaucracy

The first Han emperor, Gaozu, recruited the earliest members of the imperial civil service. In 196 B.C., he issued an edict ordering all senior provincial officials and high-ranking officials to send to the capital city all the worthy and virtuous men they knew or were aware of so that their talents could be evaluated. Those who showed the most promise might be lucky enough to receive appointments as officials. Gaozu's edict set into motion the system that chose men on the basis of ability in keeping with the teachings of Confucianism.

Later Han emperors continued and expanded on the practice initiated by Gaozu. Within a hundred years, each commandery was sending a few candidates for the civil service every year. Each commandery governor was responsible for selecting the appropriate candidates based on their proven moral standards and devotion to standard duties. In addition, each governor could also submit for every two thousand people in his commandery six to ten men familiar with Chinese literature. Historical records show that by A.D. 140, at least two hundred candidates were presenting themselves each year for inspection. All came from the interior parts of China—that is, they were true Han and not subjugated barbarians from the fringes of the empire. And all had proven that they had high moral standards and were devoted to their duties.

When Wudi came into power in 140 B.C., he made additional changes to civil service. On one hand, he banned from court scholars who were not Confucians. At the same time, however, he ordered his senior officials to nominate as civil-service candidates young men of high intelligence and integrity. In time, a quota was established: One out of every 200,000 Chinese citizens must

A QUESTION OF TRAINING

Emperor Wudi was determined to fill the government bureaucracy with talented and devoted officials. In this translation by Herbert Giles, taken from John Minford and Joseph S.M. Lau's anthology *Classic Chinese Literature*, Wudi tells his provincial officials why he needs exceptional men as officials and orders them to find and send him such men from their districts.

Exceptional work demands exceptional men. A bolting or a kicking horse may eventually become a most valuable animal. A man who is the object of the world's detestation may live to accomplish great things. As with the untractable horse, so with the infatuated man;— it is simply a question of training.

We therefore command the various district officials to search for men of brilliant and exceptional talents, to be our generals, our ministers, and our envoys to distant states.

Wudi's words reveal that a man's reputation or station in life did not bar him from becoming a great bureaucrat. Faith was placed in the rigors of education and training, both of which could turn the most "untractable" individual into the most "valuable" civil servant.

be a candidate for bureaucratic training. A senior official suggested that a school be established to prepare students to become bureaucrats. Wudi responded by creating an imperial university a few miles northwest of his capital. Known as the Grand School, or *taixue*, the university taught the five classics on which Confucianism was based: *Yijing (The Book of Changes)*, *Shujing (The Book of Documents)*, *Shijing (The Book of Odes)*, *Liji (The Book of Rites)*, and *Chunqiu (Spring and Autumn Annals)*.

But even Wudi was not yet totally committed to the new merit system, as this incident related by author and broadcaster Bamber Gascoigne in his work *The Dynasties and Treasures of China* shows:

> In 130 B.C. one of the examination candidates wrote an answer relying heavily on Legalist concepts, emphasizing the importance of an effective system of punishments and rewards. The examiners marked him bottom out of more than a hundred, but the emperor, looking through the papers, disagreed with them and awarded him top place. Within a few years the fortunate candidate was occupying the highest office in the government, and it was he who finally succeeded, where his less congenial predecessors had failed, in persuading the emperor to found an academy which would give training and employment to faithful Confucians. . . .
>
> What was established in his [Wudi's] reign was not so much Confucianism as officialdom; not so much the ideal of fearless advisers guiding a selfless and attentive ruler, as the machinery

for a self-perpetuating and potentially stifling bureaucracy; not so much the free play of well-stocked minds, which was what Confucius seems to have understood by scholarship, as a pedantic obsession with detail which was over the centuries to characterize the worst of the mandarins [a high rank of Chinese public servants].[28]

Educating Future Bureaucrats and Officials

Educating a future official meant training the intellect and instilling moral principles. The candidates were trained first to be scholars and then to be administrators. This kind of training required a very special kind of teacher known as *boshi*, or scholar of great knowledge. Each *boshi* assigned to teach an ancient text had disciples. The *boshi* were viewed as masters. They did not pass their wisdom directly to the university students. Instead, they passed their teachings to their disciples, who passed them on to the students.

When Wudi created the university, he allowed only fifty students to attend. But, as time passed, the number of students kept growing. By the time the Western Han dynasty came to an end, about three thousand students were studying at the university. The number continued to grow until under the Eastern Han it reached upwards of ten thousand.

Candidates had to take and pass complex exams that tested how well they understood the classic works of Confucius. Senior civil servants usually conducted the examinations. But sometimes the emperor himself questioned the men and judged their answers. These ancient exams formed the basis

Emperor Wudi (far left) receives a letter in front of his palace.

of Chinese civil service exams well into the twentieth century.

Archaeologists have found some evidence regarding the exams. They have unearthed histories of the period, for example, that record the number of officials whose careers started when the results of their initial tests of selection proved their fitness to serve in one of the ranks of civil service. Archaeologists also found a valuable fragment of the Han laws that contains a reference to the testing of seventeen-year-olds to determine how proficient they were at certain types of reading and writing. However, scholars still have a lot to learn about the ancient civil service and its processes. Historians still are not sure exactly what topics were included in the exams, how the topics were chosen, or whether the candidates wrote their answers to the questions or gave their answers verbally.

Education Spreads to the Provinces

In time, official schools modeled after the Grand School opened in the main town of each commandery. At the head of each school was a director who had studied at the Grand School and who taught the students at least one of the classic works of Chinese philosophy. The chief purpose of the schools was the same as that of education in general—to provide suitable recruits for the civil service. As the schools trained all students in the same Confucian concepts and philosophies, they encouraged Chinese cultural unification and sameness.

Many of the pupils who attended the commandery schools entered local government. Some became state officials. There were many cases of prominent men who grew up in rural areas or in provincial towns. Exceptionally intelligent or clever commandery school pupils might be selected to go to the capital city, where they could attend classes with the sons of high officials. But, once their education was over, most returned to their home province. They came home different than when they left. No longer were they unsophisticated countrymen. Now they were officials with authority who spoke and carried themselves with pride.

The higher-ranked bureaucracy of the central government was not impressed with most provincial officials. They considered them no more than clerks and looked down on them. But a provincial official did not have to remain a provincial official forever. He could rise to an office in central government by becoming head of one of the nine ministries, or departments, or by holding one of the two more senior posts. At these levels, his duties would be very different from those of a clerk or provincial civil servant. He would be connected to those who were creating policies and making administrative decisions that might affect the entire empire.

Getting a Post

Once a candidate was presented and accepted as possessing the necessary powers of intellect, he joined others waiting at court hoping to be assigned to a vacancy. At times, as many as a thousand men stood in a group just waiting to be selected. Some offered their services as an extra adviser or as a courtier. To safeguard against corruption, a candidate could not fill a vacancy in his home district. Even if a man found an acceptable vacancy and was hired to fill it, he still had to prove himself. New officials were hired on probation for one year. If they performed well during that year of service, their appointment would be confirmed.

The government wanted to ensure that no official became overconfident or took his position for granted. So, every official's performance was reviewed every three years. Provincial authorities had to submit reports and accounts covering their area of responsibility. These reports, which became a major and long-lasting feature of Chinese civil service, often led to promotion or demotion. Archaeologists have unearthed evidence of these reports. According to their findings, a report named the official, recorded his age and height, identified his position and how long he had held it, indicated how far away he worked from his native home, and graded the quality of his services as high, medium, or low. The report also indicated how familiar the official was with the laws and included a certificate of his ability to read, write, and manage accounts.

Bureaucrats and Officials Gained Prestige and Privileges

Although proven intellect was a primary qualification for appointment, neither intelligence nor wealth could make a man a member of the bureaucracy if he was not a

A DEVOTED OFFICIAL

In the *Records of the Grand Historian*, Sima Qian writes about an official named Chi An. According to Sima Qian, Chi An's career as an official began when his father recommended him for the position of mounted guard to the heir to the throne. It did not take Chi An long to better his position and rise through the ranks of the bureaucracy.

> Chi An possesses the depth of devotion to the empire that the Han sought in their officials. In executing his duties and governing the people he valued honesty and serenity, seeking worthy assistants and secretaries and leaving them to do as they saw fit. In his administration he demanded only that the general spirit of his directives be carried out and never made a fuss over minor details. . . .
>
> The emperor, hearing of his success, summoned him to court and appointed him master of titles chief commandant, promoting him to one of the nine highest offices in the government. . . .
>
> Chi An was by nature very haughty. . . . Those who took his fancy he treated very well, but those who didn't he could not even bear to see. . . . On the other hand he was fond of learning and liked to travel about doing daring and generous things for others, and his conduct was always above reproach. . . .
>
> The emperor at this time was busy summoning scholars and Confucians to court and telling them, "I want to do thus-and-so. I want to do thus-and-so." Commenting on this Chi An said to the emperor, "On

Confucian. The need for officials was great. The number of men considered suitable for the position was not. There were many reasons to become an official or bureaucrat. Not the least of the benefits were a good salary, a host of valuable social and legal privileges, and varying amounts of prestige.

Officials and bureaucrats were revered. Bureaucrat scholars, known as mandarins, became the premier class in China. They were proud of their situation and respected by other members of society. They were viewed as pillars of the community and, throughout much of China's history, remained the most prestigious and influential people in the community. In addition, they enjoyed such privileges as not having to join the military, being exempt from labor serthe surface Your Majesty is practicing benevolence and righteousness, but in your heart you have too many desires. How do you ever expect to imitate the rule of the sage emperors Yao and Shun in this way?"

The emperor sat in silence, his face flushed with anger, and then dismissed the court. The other high officials were all terrified of what would happen to Chi An. . . .

Later, some of the officials reproached Chi An for his behavior, but he replied, "Since the Son of Heaven has gone to the trouble of appointing us as his officials and aides, what business have we in simply flattering his whims and agreeing with whatever he says, deliberately leading him on to unrighteous deeds? Now that we occupy these posts, no matter how much we may value our own safety, we cannot allow the court to suffer disgrace, can we?"

"What sort of man is Chi An anyway?" the emperor asked, to which Chuang Chu replied, "As long as he is employed in some ordinary post as an official, he will do no better than the average person. But if he were called upon to assist a young ruler or guard a city against attack, then no temptation could sway him from his duty, no amount of entreaty could make him abandon his post. Even the bravest men of antiquity . . . could not shake his determination!"

"Yes," said the emperor. "In ancient times there were ministers who were deemed worthy to be called the guardians of the altars of the nations. And men like Chi An come near to deserving the same appellation."

vice, having a day off every five days, and being able to take sick leave if they fell ill.

Grade and privilege went hand in hand, and the difference between the status of a senior and a junior official was as great as it was obvious to the public. An official did not have to wait for his performance record to be completed to be promoted. He could be promoted at any time. However, officials posted close to the central government or with good family connections stood a better chance of advancing than did the average official. Some officials were promoted after they completed their specified period of service. Each civil service post carried a grade based on earnings. A promotion generally meant going up to the next highest grade. Occasionally, an imperial edict made it possible for some extremely exceptional or especially lucky officials to advance up several grades.

As an official rose in rank or grade, so did his prestige and his rewards. Most officials were paid partly in coin and partly in goods. Generally, though, earnings were described in terms of yearly allowance of grain and varied greatly. A low-grade official might earn as much as twenty times less than a highly placed official. Officials who grew old and retired honorably from a post often were rewarded with cash bonuses or valuable bolts of silk. Some even received pensions.

A Very Regimented Bureaucracy

According to an imperial edict issued in 144 B.C., officials were the leaders of the peo-ple, and it was "right and proper that the carriages they ride in and the robes they wear should correspond to the degrees of their dignity."[29] It was easy to identify an official's rank and office because each office had its own emblem. The emblems varied according to grade; gold, silver, and bronze seals decked with purple, blue, black, and yellow ribbon indicated position and salary. Rank was important because it determined what place the official held in society and in which activities of public life he could take part.

The more junior officials conducted most of their work in offices. There, they received reports from their colleagues, drafted reports on their work, and prepared suggestions to submit to their superiors. They also inter-

A bronze model of a Han horse carriage with driver and attendant.

viewed people, judged cases brought before them for arbitration, and kept records of the taxes that had been levied. Their offices had imposing gateways, large courtyards, and shaded apartments. Officials wanted the offices to look as much as possible like the homes of important townsmen. They carefully laid out the offices to impress visitors and make them aware that officials led a venerable life accompanied by privileges and filled with duties.

Each official had his place in society and in the service of his emperor. High officials were expected to dress and travel according to their rank. It did not matter how many servants or slaves waited on an official or took care of his daily needs. He knew his place in respect to officials whose rank was

THE IMPORTANCE OF CONFUCIANISM TO THE BUREAUCRAT AND SCHOLAR

In his highly acclaimed work *China: A Macro History,* historian and author Ray Huang describes two ways in which the Han government's devotion to Confucian classics and principles directly influenced what scholars and bureaucrats learned and where their loyalties rested.

Learned men found few outlets for their talent other than governmental service. Knowledge for its own sake was not encouraged at all. . . . Stone tablets erected in front of the imperial university in A.D. 175, on which were engraved the text of six Confucian classics, daily attracted scholars and students arriving in more than 1,000 carriages. Their thirst was for a knowledge already engraved on the stone surface.

The entry of men versed in Confucian studies into the civil bureaucracy occurred first in the "recommendation system" under Wudi of the Former Han. Each province was to "elect" a man who was noted for being filial pious and another man for being incorruptible. As the system gradually became institutionalized during the Later Han, a single nominee was supposed to combine the two virtues of *xiaolian* or "filial pious and incorruptible." In each round of selection one supposedly represented 200,000 people. The choice could hardly be objective. Nor could the nominees be admitted to a deliberating assembly to deal with issues of national interest. They were given individual offices. The process in reality bonded the beneficiaries to the provincial of officials who had nominated them, creating private connections that weighed heavier than public functions.

higher than his own. No one had to tell him he was inferior to higher-ranking officials and was expected to serve them. There were inflexible rules of protocol that set down precisely how he and other officials were to behave toward one another. Junior and senior colleagues, for example, did not address one another in the same way. Established styles dictated exactly how each was to address the other. The same was true of written communications. An official framed his communications to a higher-ranked official differently than he did to someone at the same level or lower.

The emperor could present twenty orders of privilege for merit. The top twelve went to government officials. The holder of the highest order outranked everyone except the emperor and his immediate family. Because of his high rank, he could collect taxes from households in territory chosen for him. With rank came certain expectations and duties. Some of the highest-ranking officials, for example, had to attend imperial audiences and occasions where proceedings were governed by strict rules of the court. The officials who attended these occasions were carried to the palace in carriages of the style to which they were entitled. They were expected to arrive at a certain gate at a specified time. They were expected to wear their seals and the ribbons of their office and to be dressed in the proper robes and headdress. They left their carriages at the gate and walked the rest of the way. Walking from the carriage to the presence of the emperor symbolized respect, humility, and devotion to the state. It showed the court that the official truly appreciated the honor being bestowed on him and that he was determined to serve his emperor to the best of his ability. This attitude and ritual show of devotion, along with the Han system of civil service examinations based on the five Confucian classics, became fundamental characteristics of the Chinese civilization.

CHAPTER SIX

AGRICULTURE AND PEASANT FARMERS

During Han times, about 90 percent of the Chinese were peasant farmers who lived in the countryside. Even though these rural peasants were important to the very survival of the dynasty, not as much is known about them as about the nobility or the upper class. A reason for this is offered by Michele Pirazzoli-t'Serstevens in her work *The Han Dynasty:*

> The Han period is . . . at once an age of consolidation, of change, and of experiment; in four centuries the immense effort devoted to agriculture, the improvement and diffusion in the field of technology, and great movements of population totally transformed the economic scene. . . .The available information concerns mainly the intellectual and political elite. The Han historian did not write about peasants, artisans or small traders, classes that, in his view, had no history. Archaeology makes up in part for the silence of the texts; nevertheless, in so far as we can apprehend it, Han civilization remains that of the prosperous classes who gravitated round the court, held the best appointments in government, and possessed rich estates.[30]

Nonetheless, from the sources available to them, including Han tombs, archaeologists and historians have been able to paint a fair picture of the life of the rural peasant under Han rule. All agree that while the peasant farmer played an important role during the Han dynasty, he reaped few rewards. Most would agree with sinologist Michael Loewe that "The peasant was unconnected by birth with the houses of the great, and he rarely possessed resources on which he could call. For much of the Han period, he existed in a state of uncertainty, often in conditions of distress or penury [poverty]."[31]

A Hard Way of Life

From one end of China to another, Han peasant farmers built their homes and plowed their fields in the same way. Those who married generally had two or three children, and the entire family worked in the fields at one time or another. Their life was very different from that of the royal or wealthy urban dweller.

Peasant farmers generally grew crops, drained swamps, dammed streams, and built irrigation canals. For the most part, they spent their days in the repetitive and never-ending seasonal tasks of plowing, sowing, hoeing, and watering their crops of wheat,

A peasant farmer guides his ox-drawn plow through the earth.

millet, and rice. Then they would wait for months to find out whether the crops would survive and, if they did, how large their harvest would be. Their main job was to produce the grain and hemp that for Han China were the necessities of life. The Han used the grain for food and the hemp for clothing. The peasants' life was hard and their reward was small. Often, several families had to share one house and jointly work the land, which, more often than not, they did not even own.

According to Chinese tradition, eight families with plots of land bordering each other found peace, happiness, and success working the separate plots as one communal plot. If the families joined forces and worked their plots together, they could produce not only what they themselves needed but what the nobility needed as well. After all, nobles and the wealthy could not be expected to work in the fields; they did not

perform manual labor. Many farm families had difficulty producing enough on their small plots of land to put sufficient food on their tables. The only way they could produce enough to feed themselves and pay tribute to the landowners and aristocracy as well was to work cooperatively with other farm families. Living independently on their own farms was a luxury they could not afford. In addition, they needed each other to be able to create effective irrigation systems or build dikes to protect their fields in the event of drought or floods.

Poverty and hard work were the only way of life the Chinese peasant knew. The peasant had to pay taxes, serve in the army, and work for a certain number of days each year on roads, canals, or other public works. In 178 B.C. a Chinese official wrote this petition to Emperor Wendi describing the hardships endured by a typical Han peasant family of five:

GRAIN OVER GOLD

In 178 B.C., the Han statesman Chao Cuo (not related to the agriculturist Chao Kuo) offered some suggestions as to how to make the people devote themselves to agriculture. In this part of his long discourse, which is reproduced in William Theodore de Bary and Irene Bloom's *Sources of Chinese Tradition* and is taken from Han historian Ban Gu's *History of the [Former] Han Dynasty*, Chao Cuo explains that an enlightened ruler will understand that grain is more important than jewels and, by enhancing its value, will increase the people's devotion to producing it.

An enlightened ruler . . . will encourage his people in agriculture and sericulture [the raising of silkworms], lighten the poll tax and other levies, increase his stores of supplies and fill his granaries in preparation for flood and drought. Thereby he can keep and care for his people. . . .

Now pearls, jewels, gold, and silver can neither allay hunger nor keep out the cold. . . .

Grains and fibers, on the other hand, are produced from the land, nurtured through the seasons, and harvested with labor; they cannot be gotten in a day. Several measures of grain or cloth are too heavy for an average man to carry and so provide no reward for crime or evil. Yet if people go without them for one day they will face hunger and cold. Therefore an enlightened ruler esteems the five grains and despises gold and jewels. . . .

Under the present circumstances there is nothing more urgently needed than to make the people devote themselves to agriculture. To accomplish this one must enhance the value of grain.

A laborer drives his ox to till wet soil in preparation for sowing rice.

In spring they plough, in summer they weed, in autumn they reap, in winter they gather in. They also have to cut wood for the winter, repair public buildings and engage in many other public works. . . . In spring they are exposed to the biting wind and dust; in summer they are subjected to the burning sun; numbed by the autumn rain, they shiver in winter. They have not a single day of rest in the whole year. And in this life of toil they must also find time for their family duties: accompanying departing members, receiving those who arrive, going to funerals, visiting the sick, caring for orphans and bringing up their children. They are harassed by a thousand chores, and further overwhelmed by natural disasters—drought or floods. They must submit to the injunctions of a too-hurried government, unseasonable collection of taxes, orders given in the morning and countermanded in the evening. So those who have some property sell it at half its value; those who own nothing borrow and undertake to repay twice the amount, so that finally the peasant is often obliged to sell all his property, his fields, his house and sometimes even his children and grandchildren to settle his debts.[32]

Daily Life

Under some Han rulers, peasant farmers could own their plots of land, but under others they had to rent the plots they worked from nobles or wealthy landowners. The more land a peasant farmer had, the more secure he was. The standard measure of land was a *mu*, a long strip about four and a half feet wide by eleven hundred feet long. The peasant who owned a 100-*mu* plot of land clearly was better off than one who owned a 10-*mu* plot. But it was all relative. The farmer who owned the 10-*mu* plot was more secure than the farmer who rented his land and had to surrender part of his harvest to a landlord. Worst off of all, however, was the farm laborer hired just for the season.

Most peasant farmers—even those who lived in the most fertile regions of China—barely managed to survive. Home for the farmer and his family usually was a one-room house with a dirt floor. There was little or no furniture. If he rented the land he worked, he had to give up to half of his crop to the landlord who owned the fields and

An earthenware model of a Chinese fisherman preparing his catch for sale.

give another percentage to the government for taxes. Even if he owned the land, he still had to pay part of his crop as taxes. Either way, there was not much left for him or his family. Their meals usually consisted of wheat or millet cakes or something else made with grain. Sometimes they had homegrown vegetables such as beans or turnips. And every once in a while, there might be some fruit for dessert. Often, to be able to have food to feed his family, the peasant had to trap small animals or catch fish. Of course, there was a good chance that he would have to pay a tax on the fish.

To add to his burden, the peasant had to spend a certain amount of time each year in the government's labor corps. Michael Loewe, in his book *Everyday Life in Early Imperial China During the Han Period,* concludes that "many a peasant must have found himself working from time to time as a transport man on the rivers or canals; as a miner in the state-owned iron and salt mines; as a road-builder preparing highways for the emperor's progress; or on any other project that authority deemed necessary."[33] The peasant had no choice. He went where the government sent him and stayed for as long as the government demanded.

The Yield of the Land

Family was important to the peasant farmer for practical reasons. It was almost impossible for one person to work the land and produce a decent crop. A family working together cooperatively, however, was more likely to accomplish what had to be done. The typical plot of land was small—probably about eleven acres. Normally, farmers like to let a field go unplanted from time to time so that the land can renew itself. But the plots of the Han peasants were too small to let an entire field sit for a year without being planted. Instead, each year they rotated furrowing and the intervening ridges.

The farmers grew a number of different kinds of grains, depending on the climate and the soil of the area in which they lived. Wheat or millet was the most common grain in the northern provinces. Barley was the most common in the far northwest. Tea, cotton, and sugar had not yet become major crops. The grain the farmers produced was used for food. But that was not its only use; alcohol was distilled from it as well for religious functions and other celebrations.

In the north, the terrain was mountainous and covered with a rich, yellow soil called loess. Chinese farmers needed to make the most of this fertile land, so they cut long, narrow fields called terraces into the hillsides. They grew their grain in these terraces. In the south, where the Yangtze River irrigated the valleys and beyond, the farmers grew rice in flooded paddy fields. In both the south and the north, some farmers grew chestnut, date, and citrus fruit trees. In some areas, farm laborers helped maintain the lac trees that produced the lacquer used for decoration by the wealthy. They also cultivated the mulberry orchards where the silkworm fed. Before the Han came into power, most silk production was confined to the center of the country around the Yellow River region. Under the Han, it expanded outward to frontier provinces.

Depending on the lay of the land and the climate of an area, a farmer might be able to breed or graze horses, cattle, sheep, or pigs. Drawings in an A.D. 103 tomb, for example, reveal a plowman with two oxen and a shepherd with sheep. A red pottery model

WHAT IS TO BLAME
FOR POOR HARVESTS?

Emperor Wen, who ruled from about 180 to 157 B.C., was an enlightened ruler who recognized the value of grain. Concerned that not enough grain was available to feed his people, he issued a policy that gave out honorary court ranks and withdrew penalties in exchange for gifts of grain. He thought this would increase the importance his people put on grain, which in turn would stimulate them to produce more. In this selection from William Theodore de Bary and Irene Bloom's *Sources of Chinese Tradition*, taken from Han historian Ban Gu's *History of the [Former] Han Dynasty*, Wen states his concern about the shortage of food and questions why it exists and who is to blame for it.

For the past several years there have been no good harvests, and our people have suffered the calamities of flood, drought, and pestilence. We are deeply grieved by this, but being ignorant and unenlightened, we have been unable to discover where the blame lies. We have considered whether our administration has been guilty of some error or our actions of some sort. Have we failed to follow the Way of Heaven or to obtain the benefits of Earth? Have we caused disharmony in human affairs or neglected the gods that they do not accept our offerings? What brought on these things? Have the provisions for our officials been too lavish or have we indulged in too many unprofitable affairs? Why is the food of the people so scarce? When the fields are surveyed, they have not decreased, and when the people are counted they have not grown in number, so that the amount of land for each person is the same as before or even greater. And yet there is a drastic shortage of food. Where does the blame lie? Is it that too many people pursue secondary activities to the detriment of agriculture? Is it that too much grain is used to make wine or too many domestic animals are being raised? I have been unable to attain a proper balance between important and unimportant affairs. Let this matter be debated by the chancellor, the nobles, the high officials, and learned doctors. Let all exhaust their efforts and ponder deeply whether there is some way to aid the people. Let nothing be concealed from us!

Han burial models; from left, a milling shed, a stove, and an outhouse beside a penned pig.

found in the same tomb depicts a sheep pen with a child riding on the back of one of the sheep and a pigsty with a stairway leading to an upper chamber probably used as a lavatory. The sheep provided mutton for food, and their fleeces could be shaped into warm garments.

A few peasants kept fish farms. Others maintained timber woods or bamboo groves. In addition to staples like grain, some peasants also grew peaches, plums, and melons; hemp for rope and textile fiber; and bamboo to be used for construction, writing material, water pipes, chopsticks, and other common items.

Watering the Fields and Working the Land

No matter what crop the rural Han peasant grew on his small plot of land, he had to make sure that it got the proper amount of water. Controlling the supply of water to the crops was an endless and backbreaking job. To maintain a steady and constant sup-

ply to their fields, the peasants had to lift water from wells or irrigation channels. Most of the time they got the water from wells and brought it to the fields in buckets. The process was simple, but the work involved was strenuous. Over the well was a vertical support that held a pole with a bucket attached to the end. The farmer lowered the pole and filled the bucket with water from the well. Then, he fitted a heavy weight at the opposite end of the pole to raise the filled bucket out of the well, allowing the peasant to take it off the pole and transport it to the field. Not all wells were the same. Archaeologists have found different models of wells buried in Han tombs. Some were fitted with a protective housing and a roof and had a pulley built in so that buckets could be raised or lowered by rope.

Some farmers dug irrigation channels below the level of their fields, which they filled with water. Using primitive irrigation machines that they operated manually, they raised the water. Beginning around A.D. 100, the peasants began using a more sophisticated machine—a square-pallet chain pump—to cut down on the manual labor. Later, animal power or waterpower was used instead of human power to pump the water.

Making Farming Easier

Under the Han, farm tools and farming techniques were improved. There was good reason for this: The greater numbers of people living in the northwest, especially in the Western Han capital of Chang'an, required greater amounts of food. Models of what is known as the rotary winnowing fan have been found in Han tombs, most made of pottery and with miniature working parts. One such earthen-work model, for example,

A FARMING CALENDAR

Ts'ui Shih lived from about A.D. 100 to 170. Archaeologists found fragments of a short text written by him that reveals the month-by-month farming activities of a family from northeast China over the course of a year. The following is an adapted version of the monthly breakdown of the tasks identified by Ts'ui Shih.

First month (beginning on the fourth or fifth of February on a Western calendar): Transplant trees; sow melons, gourds, onions, and garlic; sweep up decayed leaves; manure the fields; prune the trees; break up heavy ground; sow crops; pay dutiful visits to social superiors; brew liquor; preserve foods

Second month: Present offerings of leeks and eggs to the lord of the soil and the spirits of the seasons; practice archery; repair gates and doors for the protection of the household; break up good arable land; sow crops; nurture and watch over silkworms; brew liquor; preserve foods

Third month: Practice archery; repair gates and doors for the protection of the household; break up light sandy soils; sow crops; nurture and watch over silkworms; brew liquor; preserve foods; replaster walls of the house; apply fresh coat of lacquer where needed

Fourth month: Break up light sandy soils; sow crops; nurture and watch over silkworms; replaster walls of the house; apply fresh coat of lacquer where needed

showed two farmworkers using these machines to clean rice. A figure seated on his heels works the husker, a pedal-powered device that slams a hammer down on the rice to smash the outer coverings of the grain. The rice is then funneled into the top of the winnower, where a second figure turns a crank that powers a fan that blows away the hull debris. The cleaned rice pours out through the opening in front. Archaeologists believe that the Chinese used cranks in machinery several centuries before these simple tools were known in Europe.

Some major improvements in farming began around 100 B.C. Historians believe that a skilled agriculturalist named Chao Kuo was responsible for many of these, including a change in how Han farmers planted their

Fifth month: Break up light sandy soils; cut hay; sow crops; collect herbs; compound drugs; sleep in a separate room from a spouse because yin and yang were locked in combat; nurture and watch over silkworms; brew liquor; preserve foods; lay in a supply of food and firewood; buy a supply of wheat-bran; dry and store wheat-bran in jars; replaster walls of the house; apply fresh coat of lacquer where needed

Sixth month: Break up light sandy soils; hoe; sow crops; spin textiles; brew liquor; preserve foods

Seventh month: Break up light sandy soils; sow crops; wash old clothes; cut new clothes; dye silk cloth; brew liquor; preserve foods

Eighth month: Present offerings of leeks and eggs to the lord of the soil and the spirits of the seasons; reverently present millet and piglets to the ancestral graves; cut hay; sow crops; wash old clothes; cut new clothes; dye silk cloth; brew liquor; preserve foods

Ninth month: Check the state of weapons; provide for the needs of the orphans, widows, and sick members of clan in the coming winter; wash old clothes; cut new clothes; dye silk cloth; brew liquor; preserve foods; repair granaries and storage pits

Tenth month: Work hemp; fashion sandals; brew liquor; preserve foods

Eleventh month: Brew liquor; preserve foods

Twelfth month: Perform rites in honor of spirits and ancestors; pay dutiful visits to social superiors; brew liquor; preserve foods; assemble plow for the coming year's work; feed the oxen to their fill.

fields. Traditionally, farmers stood in low trenches and tossed the seed upward onto a six-foot-wide *mu*. Chao Kuo had them, instead, stand on ridges and scatter the seed downward in regular lines along furrows. Planting the seed this way was not only easier but resulted in a crop yield that was similar from year to year. Another benefit was that the system of alternating positions of furrows and ridges took place almost on its own. As soon as new shoots began to sprout, the farmers pulled out the weeds on the raised ridges that separated the furrows. The soil around the weeds loosened in the process and dropped into the furrows, where it helped support the new stalks that were sprouting and growing taller. The workers kept repeating the process. By midsummer, the ridges had

Peasants in the foreground plant rice in a paddy, while others in the background irrigate the field.

flattened completely and the new crop was well rooted and better able than in the past to withstand wind and drought.

There were new tools as well, although it took a while for many farm laborers to trade their traditional tools for the new ones. Han government iron foundries began producing plowshares (the cutting blades for a plow) of different sizes, from large ones that had to be pulled by a team of oxen to small, pointed ones that could be used by a single person. Most farmers followed an ancient Chinese proverb that said they should plow their land after rain to save the moisture in the ground. The new equipment made this backbreaking task much easier. One of the major inventions was a new plow that had two plowshares. Two oxen pulled the plow,

while one man led the way and two others controlled the handles.

The Backbone of the Empire

The Han government was in favor of any improvements that would increase the amount of crops the peasant farmers produced. The government openly acknowledged that the rural peasant farmers were the backbone of the empire and that the survival of the entire country depended on agriculture. "The world is based on agriculture," Han emperors declared in several edicts. Because the Han government's system of revenues was based on the successful use of land, the government was dependent in great part on the peasant. A government could fall from power if it acted in a way that caused the peasants to abandon their small pieces of land or made it impossible for them to work the land for even a short period of time.

For the Han, agriculture was what distinguished the Chinese from the alien peoples, the "barbarians," outside the walls of their empire. They believed that agriculture was the reason Chinese families led a settled form of life under the protection of the emperor's government. In their view, without agriculture, the Chinese would be no different from the nomad peoples outside the walls who spent their lives going from pasture to pasture trying to make a living.

REFLECTIONS OF THE PAST

In 1972, a major archaeological event occurred in China. Workers on a hospital project outside Changsha, the capital of Hunan province, came across a sixty-five-foot-high burial mound. They had no inkling that within the burial mound was the first complete human body from ancient times ever to be unearthed in China. Archaeologists found the body resting under twenty layers of silk in a casket deep in the tomb. The heavy outer coffins the archaeologists had pried open before reaching the casket were a major find in themselves, full of Han dynasty silks, lacquerware, wooden statuettes, musical instruments, and paintings. When they finally uncovered the innermost casket and unwrapped the many layers of silk that enfolded the body, the female body, remarkably free of decay, was revealed. At first, the archaeologists thought they had found the wife of the first Marquis of Tai. Later, some scholars identified her instead as Lady Ch'eng. Lady Ch'eng had been a consort of Emperor Ching, who ruled China from 156 B.C. to 141 B.C., and the mother of three of the emperor's sons. This article appeared two years later in *National Geographic*. It offers insights into the life and death of the aristocrat buried in the tomb and discusses the customs and traditions of her dynasty:

One soft summer morning she rose early, donned a silk gown, and strolled about the gardens, moving slowly with the aid of a walking stick. She had more than a little reason for happiness. Surrounded by all the trappings of wealth, she also basked in the esteem granted to older women of her class. A servant offered her fresh melon on a lacquer plate. She ate and rested. Then a kernel of fire in her chest expanded into massive pain. Unconsciousness enveloped her, and she died. Her story sounds contemporary but it is not. The world on which the noblewoman closed her eyes was that of China early in the Han Dynasty, more than 2,100 years ago. Her mourners believed that her immortality hinged on how well they observed funeral rituals and preserved her mortal form, and they went to extraordinary lengths. How well they succeeded only now has become known, and the details are so rich that events of the lady's last day seem to unreel before our eyes. . . . Whoever the aristocratic woman was, she breathed the air of peace. During the tombed according to the Chinese *Book of Rites*.[34]

At the end of 1973, excavators found a smaller tomb in a layer below that of the noblewoman. Archeologists believe the tomb was the noblewoman's son's. The tomb contained more than seventeen hundred funerary goods, including a wooden slip dated early 168 B.C. Among the textiles, lacquer objects, weapons, and other goods were more than thirty texts written between 231 B.C. and the first twenty or thirty years of the Han dynasty. No wonder archaeologists and historians say that tombs like these have opened a window into the dynamic world of the Han dynasty. Along with histories transcribed by linguists and historians, the tombs have made it possible to delve into the social conditions, manners, and customs of a dynasty that ceased to exist nearly two thousand years ago.

Excellence in Many Fields

By the end of the first century B.C., Han scholars and scientists had observed sunspots, something the Europeans would not do until the late 1500s or early 1600s. The Han also had accurately determined the length of the calendar year. They had a lunar calendar that would be consulted into the twentieth century.

In the second century A.D., the Eastern Han ruled China. By that time, China had caught up with, and in some areas had gone well beyond, Europe and West Asia in science and technology. The Han alone had made amazing contributions. During that century, the Chinese technique for making porcelain matured and Chuko Liang invented the wheelbarrow.

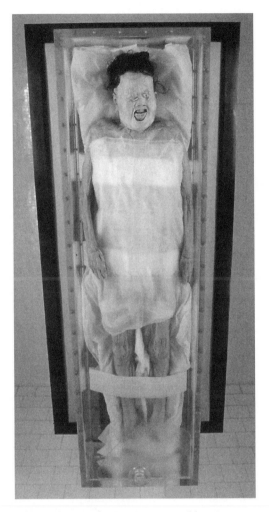

The mummified body of a Han noblewoman, whose identity is a source of scholarly debate.

second century B.C., Han emperors finally ended rebellions, and the unified nation entered a golden age. The Chinese could pause to take pride in their civilization. . . . Following ancient teachings, they paid high honor to the family—both living and dead. And so the lady and her belongings were meticulously en-

Beautiful figurines, such as this earthenware dancer, are only part of the rich cultural legacy of the Han.

Another Han legacy that century was paper. Historical records show that in A.D. 105 a eunuch who was an official of the Imperial Court during the Eastern Han told Emperor Ho Di about paper. An official history written several centuries later explained why paper was important and how it was made:

> In ancient times writing was generally on bamboo or on pieces of silk, which were then called ji. But silk being expensive and bamboo heavy,

these two materials were not convenient. Then Tsai Lun thought of using tree bark, hemp, rags, and fish nets. In 105 he made a report to the emperor on the process of papermaking, and received high praise for his ability. From this time paper has been in use everywhere and is called the "paper of Marquis Tsai."[35]

Less than thirty years later—in A.D. 132 —a royal Han astronomer and mathematician, Zhang Heng, invented an eight-feet-wide primitive seismograph made of bronze. Zhang Heng's invention signaled earthquakes as far away as several hundred miles. It indicated the direction of the earthquake by dropping a bronze ball from the mouth of a dragon into the mouth of a toad that sat below it. The "technology" was based on an inverted pendulum inside a jar. When the earth shook, the pendulum tilted and fell into one of eight channels facing different ways. As the pendulum moved, it pushed a trigger that opened the dragon's jaws and ejected a corresponding ball indicating direction. According to one story, the Confucians of the capital did not like or trust Zhang Heng. So, they were very happy the day the seismograph dragon released his ball and no news of an earthquake came and no shock was felt. Their happiness ended, however, a few days later. A messenger arrived that day from northwestern China to tell everyone that an earthquake had occurred there.

A Large and Lasting Legacy

The Han left their footprint in many other areas as well. They used waterpower to grind grain and to operate a piston bellows for iron smelting. They invented the stirrup and developed a horse collar that helped horses pull harder. Their architects and engineers built the first suspension bridge, as well as major portions of the Great Wall of China. They also built numerous roads, canals, and irrigation systems, and huge, elaborate palaces and tombs that they filled with finely crafted relics and figurines that are highly valued by art collectors today. They also invented a drill that could make a hole close to five thousand feet deep. They dug mines and, in the process, discovered coal and natural gas, which they used for cooking and heating centuries before Europeans thought to do the same. They did all of these things, and passed their benefits on to future generations, long before Europeans achieved anything comparable.

In government, the Han created a bureaucracy that worked so well that it barely changed at all for the next twenty-one hundred years. More than a thousand years before modern archaeologists began classifying human history by "ages," a Han scholar divided history into the stone age, the jade age, the bronze age, and his present age when weapons were made of iron. Another Han scholar created the world's first dictionary, *Shuo Wen* (*Words Explained*), which listed the meaning and pronunciation of more than nine thousand Chinese characters.

Few would disagree with the truth of these words of historian Kenneth Scott Latourette in regard to the lasting contribution of the Han:

> The downfall of the Han did not entirely undo the work of that dynasty and its predecessor. To the ideas, the literature, and the institutions of the period later generations recurred again and again. Even in recent times, the Chinese have proudly called themselves *Han Jê* "the men of Han." No radically different political system was seriously tried until the twentieth century. The China of the next two millennia had been born.[36]

The Chinese, as well as other cultures, throughout the centuries put faith in the Han belief stated by Han historian Sima Qian in the *Records of the Historian* that the events of the past, if not forgotten, are teachings about the future. That understanding remains even today a valued legacy of the Han dynasty.

NOTES

Introduction: The Great Han Dynasty

1. Bamber Gascoigne, *The Dynasties and Treasures of China*. New York: Viking Press, 1973, pp. 75–76.
2. Thomas H. Maugh II, "2,000-Year-Old Stone Toilet Unearthed in Chinese Tomb," *Los Angeles Times*, July 27, 2000, p. B-2.
3. Michael Loewe, *Everyday Life in Early Imperial China During the Han Period 202 B.C.–A.D. 220*. New York: G.P. Putnam's Sons, 1968, p. 27.

Chapter 1: Building Foundations: Before the Han

4. Kwang-chih Chang, *The Archaeology of Ancient China*. New Haven, CT: Yale University Press. 1986, pp. 296–97.
5. Quoted in Chang, *The Archaeology of Ancient China*, pp. 340–41.
6. René Grousset, *The Rise and Splendor of the Chinese Empire*. Berkeley and Los Angeles: University of California Press, 1953, pp. 49–50.
7. Ray Huang, *China: A Macro History*. Armonk, NY: M.E. Sharpe, 1997, p. 22.
8. Brian Williams, *Ancient China*. New York: Viking Press, 1996, p. 18.

9. Quoted in Sima Qian, *Historical Records*, trans. Raymond Dawson. New York: Oxford University Press, 1994, p. 83.
10. Quoted in William Theodore de Bary and Irene Bloom, eds., *Sources of Chinese Tradition: From Earliest Times to 1600*, vol. 1. New York: Columbia University Press, 1999, p. 210.
11. Caroline Blunden and Mark Elvin, *Cultural Atlas of China*. New York: Checkmark Books, 1983, p. 83.

Chapter 2: Four Hundred Years of Power

12. John Hood, "Chang Ch'ien and Han Conquest," *History Net*, April 1966. www.thehistorynet.com.
13. "Secrets of the Great Wall of China." www.1uptravel.com.
14. Ch'en Lin, "Song: I Watered My Horse at the Long Wall Caves," in *The Columbia Book of Chinese Poetry: From Early Times to the Thirteenth Century*, trans. and ed. Burton Watson. New York: Columbia University Press, 1984, pp. 107–108.
15. Quoted in de Bary and Bloom, *Sources of Chinese Tradition*, p. 356.
16. Wang Ts'an, "Seven Sorrows," in *The Columbia Book of Chinese Poetry*, p. 106.

Chapter 3: The Orderly Underpinnings of Society

17. *The Great Learning,* in *The Chinese Classics,* vol. 1, trans. James Legge. Hong Kong: Hong Kong University Press, 1960. www.chinapage.com

18. Grousset, *The Rise and Splendor of the Chinese Empire,* pp. 49–50.

19. Raymond Dawson, ed. *The Legacy of China.* Oxford, England: Clarendon Press, 1964, p. 64.

20. Edward Craig, ed. "Article 8: Chinese Philosophy: First Millennium Syncretism," *Routledge Encyclopedia of Philosophy Online,* 2000. www. rep.rout lege.com

Chapter 4: A Single and Supreme Ruler

21. Loewe, *Everyday Life in Early Imperial China During the Han Period,* pp. 29–30.

22. Quoted in Edward H. Schafer and the Editors of Time-Life Books, *Ancient China.* New York: Time-Life Books, 1976, p. 84

23. Loewe, *Everyday Life in Early Imperial China During the Han Period,* p. 29

24. Jaime A. FlorCruz, "Archaeologist Wang Xueli Will Never Forget That May Afternoon Last," *Time International,* December 23, 1991.

25. B.K. Davis, "The Chinese Emperors' Eternal Armies," *Jade Dragon Online,* February 1998. www.jadedragon.com.

Chapter 5: A Bureaucracy Based on Merit

26. Kenneth Scott Latourette, *The Chinese: Their History and Culture.* New York: Macmillan, 1964, p. 105.

27. Confucius, *The Doctrine of the Mean,* in *The Chinese Classics.* www.chinapage.com.

28. Gascoigne, *The Dynasties and Treasure of China,* pp. 71–72.

29. Quoted in *China's Buried Kingdoms.* Alexandria, VA: Time-Life Books, 1993, p. 124.

Chapter 6: Agriculture and Peasant Farmers

30. Michele Pirazzoli-t'Serstevens, *The Han Dynasty,* trans. Janet Seligman. New York: Rizzoli International, 1982, p. 8.

31. Loewe, *Everyday Life in Early Imperial China During the Han Period,* p. 60.

32. Pirazzoli-t'Serstevens, *The Han Dynasty,* pp. 31–32.

33. Loewe, *Everyday Life in Early Imperial China During the Han Period,* p. 60.

Epilogue: Reflections of the Past

34. Alice J. Hall, "A Lady from China's Past," *National Geographic,* May 1974, pp. 660–61.

35. Silkroad Foundation, "The History of Paper." www.silk-road.com.

36. Latourette, *The Chinese,* p. 105.

CHRONOLOGY

B.C.

ca. 2000–1700

Yü founds the Xia dynasty. Pigs, dogs, goats, and sheep are domesticated in China.

ca. 1700–1000

The Shang dynasty establishes and maintains control over the settlements along the Yellow River. Around 1384 they establish a capital at Anyang with large palaces. The Shang develop a system of writing and master the use of bronze to create ritual vessels.

ca. 1000–221

Wu Wen conquers the Shang and founds the Zhou dynasty. The Zhou establish a capital at Chang'an. They develop a written legal code and use oracle bones to foretell the future. Conflicts break out, forcing the Zhou to move their capital eastward to Luoyang, resulting in two different periods of Zhou rule—Western Zhou and Eastern Zhou. Confucius, author of *The Analects*, is born during this period and teaches the importance of centralized authority and filial piety. Laozi, author of the *Dao de jing* and Master of Daoism, encourages people to live simply and according to nature.

221–210

Zhao Zheng becomes Shi huangdi ("First Emperor") of the Qin dynasty and institutes a Legalist government. China becomes unified for the first time under the Qin, who in 214 begin building the Great Wall as a defense against invasion by barbarians from the north. Shi huangdi standardizes the writing script and weights and measures. Prime Minister Li Si orders the burning of all books except religious, medical, and agricultural texts.

202–195

Gaozu overthrows the Qin and reigns as the first ruler of the Former, or Western, Han dynasty. He establishes a capital at Chang'an.

188–180

Han dowager empress Lü rules the empire.

140

Wudi ascends the throne and launches a new era in Chinese history, during which the Chinese empire expands to its greatest extent, Confucianism becomes the official state ideology, copper coins are introduced, mining is established, and the power of the central government is increased.

138
Zhang Qian sets off on his search for the Yuezhi tribe. He returns to China thirteen years later with wondrous goods from western Asia.

ca. 130
Wudi establishes a civil service system.

124
The imperial university is founded primarily to train young men to be bureaucrats and officials.

ca. 120
The Han extend the Great Wall. The Silk Road opens between China and the Parthian Empire, establishing the first cross-cultural exchanges between East and West.

102–100
Wudi's armies capture Ferghana and bring "Celestial Horses" to China for the first time.

ca. 97
Sima Qian writes the *Records of the Historian*, the first systemized and comprehensive history of China.

87
The reign of Wudi ends.

A.D.
9
The Western Han dynasty collapses.

9–23
Wang Mang usurps the power of the Han and rules as emperor of a new dynasty, the Xin.

ca. 25
Buddhism is introduced to China.

25–57
Gwangwu Di rules as the first emperor of the Later, or Eastern, Han dynasty, and moves the capital city to Luoyang.

190
Rebels burn down Luoyang.

220
The Eastern Han dynasty collapses.

FOR FURTHER READING

Anne Birrell, *Popular Songs and Ballads of Han China*. Honolulu: University of Hawaii Press, 1995. Translations and criticism of more than seventy songs and ballads of early imperial China.

Derk Bodde, *Festivals in Classical China: New Year and Other Annual Observances During the Han Dynasty, 206* B.C.–A.D. *220*. Princeton, NJ, and Hong Kong: Princeton University Press and the Chinese University of Hong Kong, 1975. Encyclopedic account of textual references to festivals during the Han period of rule.

China's Buried Kingdoms. Alexandria, VA: Time-Life Books, 1993. Traces the history and culture of the Shang, the Eastern Zhou, the Qin, and the Han. Includes interesting discussions of relevant and unusual archaeological finds.

Arthur Cotterell, *Ancient China*. New York: Alfred A. Knopf, 1994. Well-illustrated introduction to almost all aspects of ancient Chinese civilization and culture.

O.B. Duane and N. Hutchinson, *Chinese Myths and Legends*. London: Brockhampton Press, 1998. A collection of fascinating ancient Chinese myths and tales (illustrated with paintings and etchings) that provide insights into Chinese concepts of life and death.

Irene M. Franck and David M. Brownstone, *The Silk Road: A History*. New York: Facts On File, 1986. The story of the Silk Road from its beginnings, often through the words of the ancients who traveled it.

Michael Goodman and Anthony Christie, *Chinese Mythology*. New York: P. Bedrick Books, 1985. Discusses the myths and gods of ancient China and their sources.

Thomas Hoobler, *Confucianism*. New York: Facts On File, 1993. Traces the evolution of the teachings of Confucius from a social order to a religion.

Lucy Lim, ed., *Stories from China's Past: Han Dynasty Pictorial Tomb Reliefs and Archaeological Objects from Sichuan Province, People's Republic of China*. San Francisco: Chinese Culture Foundation, 1987. A catalog of about one hundred items from Sichuan province, including Han dynasty tomb reliefs, rubbings, and rare archaeological finds. Photos of the items are accompanied by essays.

Michele Pirazzoli-t'Serstevens, *The Han Dynasty*. Trans. Janet Seligman. New York: Rizzoli International, 1982. Excellent introduction to Han history.

Frank Xavier Ross, *Oracle Bones, Stars, and Wheelbarrows: Ancient Chinese Science and Technology*. Boston: Houghton Mifflin, 1982. Describes ancient Chinese achievements in such fields as astronomy, medicine, science, and engineering, including such inventions as paper, printing, gunpowder, and the compass.

Maurizio Scarpari, *Splendours of Ancient China*. London: Thames and Hudson, 2000. More than four hundred illustrations and photographs of ancient Chinese artistic and archaeological masterpieces, including buildings, works of art, cities, and landscapes. Recounts the history of the civilization and culture of ancient China from the Neolithic Age to the period of the empire.

Sima Qian, *Records of the Grand Historian: Han Dynasty II*. Vol. 2. Trans. Burton Watson. New York: Columbia University Press, 1995. Translation of the *Shiji*, Sima Qian's history of China and its neighboring countries from the ancient past to his own time.

WORKS CONSULTED

Books

Caroline Blunden and Mark Elvin, *Cultural Atlas of China*. New York: Checkmark Books, 1983. Describes textually and graphically China's natural environment, art, politics, society, language, writing, religion, medicine, mathematics, ceramics, music, theater, farming and food, and family life.

Kwang-chih Chang, *The Archaeology of Ancient China*. New Haven, CT: Yale University Press, 1986. Well-written and extremely well-documented text on Chinese archaeology by a Harvard professor of archaeology.

The Chinese Classics. Vol. 1. Trans. James Legge. Hong Kong: Hong Kong University Press, 1960. A translation of the ancient Chinese classies *The Book of History, Filial Piety, The Great Learning,* and *The Doctrine of the Mean* by a late-nineteenth-century Oxford University scholar.

Chuang Tzu, *Basic Writings*. Trans. Burton Watson. New York: Columbia University Press, 1996. Translation by a renowned translator of Chinese and Japanese of eleven chapters of the famous book written by Chuang Tzu, the ancient Chinese philosopher who was one of the earliest Daoists.

The Columbia Book of Chinese Poetry: From Early Times to the Thirteenth Century. Trans. and ed. Burton Watson. New York: Columbia University Press, 1984. An anthology of translations of the works of many different ancient and early Chinese poets, bringing to the surface the emotions and features of Chinese life.

Raymond Dawson, ed., *The Legacy of China*. Oxford, England: Clarendon Press, 1964. General account of Chinese civilization that places importance on the ancient Chinese scientific and technological achievements.

Corinne Debaine-Francfort, *The Search for Ancient China*. New York: Harry N. Abrams, 1999. Describes the birth of archaeology in China and provides vivid accounts and descriptions of major Chinese archaeological finds from the Neolithic period through the rule of the Han.

William Theodore de Bary and Irene Bloom, eds., *Sources of Chinese Tradition: From Earliest Times to 1600*. Vol. 1. New York: Columbia University Press, 1999. An anthology of translations of various ancient Chinese documents, each preceded by a concise explanatory introduction. Collectively, the writings provide important insights into the fundamentals of Chinese civilization.

Bamber Gascoigne, *The Dynasties and Treasures of China*. New York: Viking Press, 1973. A dynasty-by-dynasty portrayal of ancient Chinese arts from the Shang to the Ch'ing dynasty accompanied by an enjoyable narrative that highlights interesting details and information about each dynasty and object of art.

Marcel Granet, *Chinese Civilization*. New York: Barnes and Noble, 1951. Discussion by a recognized European sinologist of ancient Chinese civilization based on the words and works of ancient Chinese.

René Grousset, *The Rise and Splendor of the Chinese Empire*. Berkeley and Los Angeles: University of California Press, 1953. Scholarly study of the historical development and culture of the Chinese Empire.

Grant Hardy, *Worlds of Bronze and Bamboo: Sima Qian's Conquest of History*. New York: Columbia University Press, 1999. Argues that when Sima Qian wrote the *Shiji* he did not intend to produce a consistent, closed interpretation of the past.

Ray Huang, *China: A Macro History*. Armonk, NY: M.E. Sharpe, 1997. Slightly unconventional but well-written survey of Chinese history over the last several thousand years, written by a widely published Chinese author and historian.

Brian P. Katz, *Deities and Demons of the Far East*. New York: Metro Books, 1995. Fascinating overview of Far Eastern religious and mythological beliefs. The chapter on China explores Daoism, Confucianism, Mohism, and the Chinese adaptation of Buddhism, as well as the Great Ten Legendary Rulers, yin and yang, dragons, and patron gods.

Louise Kuo and Yuan-Hsi Kuo, *Chinese Folk Tales*. Millbrae, CA: Celestial Arts, 1976. Collection of Chinese tales that form the basis of Chinese folklore.

Kenneth Scott Latourette, *The Chinese: Their History and Culture*. New York: Macmillan, 1964. A review of more than three thousand years of Chinese history that outlines the course of China's development and surveys Chinese civilization.

Michael Loewe, *Crisis and Conflict in Han China, 104 B.C. to A.D. 9*. London: Allen & Unwin, 1974. A collection of essays about Han dynasty politics.

———, *Divination, Mythology, and Monarchy in Han China*. Vol. 48. New York: Cambridge University Press, 1994. Traces the changes in the ideas about rule and rulers, including how emperors and others forecast the future or divined the present.

——— *Everyday Life in Early Imperial China During the Han Period 202 B.C.– A.D. 220*. New York: G.P. Putnam's Sons, 1968. Definitive work that reads easily and describes vividly many of the day-to-day conditions of life in Han China.

John Minford and Joseph S.M. Lau, eds., *Classical Chinese Literature: An Anthology of Translations*. New York: Columbia University Press, 2000. Compilation of Chinese writings from antiquity to the Tang dynasty.

William H. Nienhauser Jr., ed., *The Grand Scribe's Records, Vol. 1: The Basic Annals of Pre-Han China by Ssu-ma Ch'ien*. Bloomington: Indiana University Press, 1994. Part of the nine-volume translation of one of the most important narratives of ancient China. Covers the seven basic annals that trace the history of the mythical and real rulers of China through the late third century B.C.

Pan Ku, *Courtier and Commoner in Ancient China: Selections from the History of the Former Han*. Trans. Burton Watson and Pan Kun. New York: Columbia University Press, 1977. Translation of selected parts of Pan Ku's *History of the*

Former Han, which served as a model for dynastic history since its appearance in the first century A.D.

J.A.G. Roberts, *A History of China. Vol. 1: Prehistory to c. 1800*. New York: St. Martin's Press, 1996. Surveys Chinese history from prehistoric times and the Shang dynasty to the end of the eighteenth century.

Edward H. Schafer and the Editors of Time-Life Books, *Ancient China*. New York: Time-Life Books, 1976. This volume from the Great Ages of Man series presents a clear and interesting overview of ancient Chinese civilization and culture.

Sima Qian, *Historical Records*. Trans. Raymond Dawson. New York: Oxford University Press, 1994. Translation by a classical Chinese scholar of the *Shiji*, the Han grand historian's history of the Chinese world from its beginnings up to the late second century B.C. Includes an introduction that examines Sima Qian in the tradition of history writing and places the Qin dynasty in a wider historical context.

Jenny F. So and Emma C. Bunker, *Traders and Raiders on China's Northern Frontier*. Seattle: University of Washington Press in association with Smithsonian's Sackler Gallery, 1995. Well-illustrated study of the cultural contribution during the Han period of the "barbarian" tribes along the northern borders of China and the trade northward.

Sun Xiaochun and Jacob Kistemaker, *Chinese Sky During the Han: The Constellations Reconstructed and Their Cultural Background Explored*. Leiden, the Netherlands: Brill Academic Publishers, 1997. Scholarly reconstruction of the Chinese sky during the rule of the Han, based on analysis of the first star catalogue in China and other sources and presented in six star maps for 100 B.C.

Nancy Lee Swann, *Pan Chao: Foremost Woman Scholar of China*. New York: Russell & Russell, 1932. Study of the background, ancestry, life, and writings of the celebrated first century A.D. Chinese Woman of letters considered the first and foremost Confucian scholar.

Robert K.G. Temple, *China: Land of Discovery and Invention*. Wellingborough, England: Patrick Stephens, 1986. A well-illustrated condensed version of Joseph Needham's multivolume history of science and technology in China.

TimeFrame 400 B.C.–A.D. 200: Empires Ascendant. Alexandria, VA: Time-Life Books, 1987. A volume from the TimeFrame series that focuses on the history and culture of several ancient empires, including China, from 400 B.C. to A.D. 200.

The Tso chuan: Selections from China's Oldest Narrative History. Trans. Burton Watson. New York: Columbia University Press, 1989. Internationally recognized translation of the most famous and influential narratives from the third-century-B.C. Chinese classic that gave an account of political, diplomatic, and military affairs from about 722 B.C. to 468 B.C.

Ch'u T'ung-csu, *Han Social Structures*. Ed. Jack Dull. Seattle: University of Washington Press, 1972. Primary sources and analysis of society during the time of the Han dynasty.

Denis C. Twitchett and Michael Loewe, eds., *The Ch'in and Han Empires, 221 B.C.–A.D. 220, Vol. 1: The Cambridge History of China*. Cambridge, England: Cambridge University Press, 1986. Old-fashioned history book that is an excellent reference.

Wang Zhongshu, *Han Civilization*. Trans. K.C. Chang et al. New Haven, CT: Yale University Press, 1982. Survey of Han archaeology based on a series of lectures.

Brian Williams, *Ancient China*. New York: Viking Press, 1996. Well-illustrated introduction to the people and culture of ancient China written for young people.

Periodicals

Jaime A. FlorCruz, "Archaeologist Wang Xueli Will Never Forget That May Afternoon Last," *Time International*, December 23, 1991.

Alice J. Hall, "A Lady from China's Past," *National Geographic*, May 1974. Description of the treasures unearthed from an early Han dynasty tomb; accompanied by a pictorial of the artifacts.

Charles Higham, "China's Terracotta Army: Silent Soldiers Guard the Breathtaking Tomb of Qin Shihuang," *Discovering Archaeology*, November/December 1999. A professor of anthropology's description and impressions of the Qin terra-cotta army unearthed in the 1970s.

Thomas H. Maugh II, "2,000-Year-Old Stone Toilet Unearthed in Chinese Tomb," *Los Angeles Times*, July 27, 2000.

Internet Sources

Chinese Empresses, Imperial Concubines Live in Unusual Palace 2000 Years Ago, Xinhua News Agency, March 7, 2001, www.xinhuanet.com

Edward Craig, ed., "Article 8: Chinese Philosophy: First Millennium Syncretism," *Routledge Encyclopedia of Philosophy Online*, 2000. www.rep.routledge.com.

B.K. Davis, "The Chinese Emperors' Eternal Armies," *Jade Dragon Online*, February 1998. www.jadedragon.com.

John Hood, "Chang Ch'ien and Han Conquest," *History Net*, April 1966. www.thehistorynet.com.

"Secrets of the Great Wall of China." www.1uptravel.com.

Silkroad Foundation, "The History of Paper." www.silk-road.com.

INDEX

ABOUT THE AUTHOR

Myra Immell was a teacher and, for twenty years, a member of the editorial staff of a major textbook publisher, where she specialized in social studies materials for grades 6 to 12. For several years, she was a freelance author, editor, and educational consultant. Currently she is a proposal writer for a leading technology provider. Mrs. Immell has edited and written a number of volumes for Greenhaven Press and Lucent Books on diverse subjects.